Praise for *Her True Worth*

"In a world full of messages telling women all the ways they're unworthy, Brittany and Cassandra have poured out much-needed truths to remind us of who we are in Christ and how He sees us."

—AMY GROESCHEL, COFOUNDER OF LIFE.CHURCH AND FOUNDER OF BRANCH15, A NONPROFIT MINISTRY PROVIDING CARE TO WOMEN

"Before a book even came to be, Brittany and Cassandra were fervently following the voice of God and breaking cycles of women feeling unworthy. Dive in deep, and allow these words to do the holy work they were written to do."

—TONI COLLIER, SPEAKER, AUTHOR, AND FOUNDER OF BROKEN CRAYONS

"Solid, biblical, a staple to have on hand for generations to come. *Her True Worth* has given us truth after beautiful truth in this important book—one every woman should own."

—LISA WHITTLE, BESTSELLING AUTHOR, BIBLE TEACHER, AND PODCAST HOST

"In a world that teaches us to measure our worth by our social media followings, achievements, and striving, *Her True Worth* gently turns us back to where our identity truly lies: in Jesus. Brittany and Cassandra empower women to remember the source of all hope and encourage us to lay down our idols in exchange for true peace in him."

—DANIELLE COKE, ILLUSTRATOR, ACTIVIST, AND FOUNDER OF OH HAPPY DANI

"*Her True Worth* is a breath of fresh air to any woman who has chosen to follow Jesus in the twenty-first century. Britt and Cass boldly speak to the struggles, hindrances, and pressures of the modern woman of faith while pointing the reader to the truth that has the power to set them free. From the new believer to the seasoned one alike; *Her True Worth* is a staple and asset to the identity formation of all women who are called by his name."

—MARIELA ROSARIO, AUTHOR AND FOUNDER OF SHE SPEAKS FIRE

"Like good friends, Cassandra and Brittany invite the woman who believes she will never measure up, to hear *truth-soaked teaching*—that guides her heart to recall the ways God has *always* seen her and who she was *always* created to be."

—JENA HOLIDAY, ILLUSTRATOR, AUTHOR, AND OWNER OF
SPOONFUL OF FAITH ILLUSTRATION AND DESIGN STUDIO

"A much-needed message for us to stop striving for worth and seeking the world's approval. Instead, Brittany and Cassandra guide us to live from the worth that's already been given to us by Jesus. A life-giving message for all to embrace!"

—ALITA REYNOLDS, PRESIDENT, WOMEN OF FAITH

"The best storytellers normalize our lived experiences and fill us with hope for the future. The women of Her True Worth understand how the robust coupling of stories and theology can lead to transformation. This book is rich in mercy and offers women an alternative to hustle culture, denial, and people-pleasing. With their history of inspiration to women everywhere, these pages are a deeper deposit of the restorative power of God to those who need it."

—ASHLEY ABERCROMBIE, AUTHOR AND PODCASTER

"The words within this book are for every woman who needs to be reminded of her worth. Brittany and Cassandra take the reader on a journey of hope and wholeness in Christ through powerful stories. You will see yourself reflected, weep, laugh, and remember just how much you are loved by God."

—BETHNY RICKS, SPEAKER, AUTHOR, AND
FAITH-BASED LEADERSHIP EXPERT

"One of the greatest lies the enemy tempts us with is to think that our worth as God's image bearers is somehow up for the taking. We get lost in fighting for value and acceptance, while missing God's divine invitation to not only live from our true identity—but our worth. In *Her True Worth* you'll find a call and an invitation to finally break free from the lie that your worth is found in anything other than Christ alone."

—ALEXANDRA HOOVER, MINISTRY LEADER AND AUTHOR OF
EYES UP: HOW TO TRUST GOD'S HEART BY TRACING HIS HAND

"Brittany Maher and Cassandra Speer have put their finger on the single greatest heart cry of women today. With laser-like focus, brilliant clarity, and relatable stories from their own lives, they explain why so few of us feel deeply settled in the truth of our own worth, and that we don't have to live this way anymore. For anyone who struggles with insecurity, self-doubt, people-pleasing, or comparison, this book has good news for you."

—SHARON HODDE MILLER, AUTHOR OF *FREE OF ME:
WHY LIFE IS BETTER WHEN IT'S NOT ABOUT YOU*

"In a world where we are relentlessly bombarded with messages that communicate to us that we aren't enough, Cass and Britt function in tandem in the most symbiotically beautiful way to expose the lies of the enemy and encourage us to run full speed ahead into the race God has called each of us to run. I found myself, at once restful yet prepared to take what is rightfully mine. This timely message is a gift to us all."

—KENNESHA N. BUYCKS, AUTHOR AND
FOUNDER OF RESTORATION HOUSE

her *true* worth

her
true
worth

Breaking Free from a Culture of Selfies,
Side Hustles, and People Pleasing to
Embrace Your True Identity in Christ

Brittany Maher & Cassandra Speer
Leaders of the Her True Worth Community

NELSON
BOOKS

An Imprint of Thomas Nelson

Published in Nashville, Tennessee, by Nelson Books, an imprint of Thomas Nelson. Nelson Books and Thomas Nelson are registered trademarks of HarperCollins Christian Publishing, Inc.

Published in association with The Bindery Agency, www.TheBinderyAgency.com.

Thomas Nelson titles may be purchased in bulk for educational, business, fundraising, or sales promotional use. For information, please e-mail SpecialMarkets@ThomasNelson.com.

Unless otherwise noted, Scripture quotations taken from The Holy Bible, New International Version®, NIV®. Copyright © 1973, 1978, 1984, 2011 by Biblica, Inc.® Used by permission of Zondervan. All rights reserved worldwide. www.Zondervan.com. The "NIV" and "New International Version" are trademarks registered in the United States Patent and Trademark Office by Biblica, Inc.®

Scripture quotations marked ESV are taken from the ESV® Bible (The Holy Bible, English Standard Version®). Copyright © 2001 by Crossway, a publishing ministry of Good News Publishers. Used by permission. All rights reserved.

Scripture quotations marked NASB are taken from the New American Standard Bible® (NASB). Copyright © 1960, 1962, 1963, 1968, 1971, 1972, 1973, 1975, 1977, 1995, 2020 by The Lockman Foundation. Used by permission. www.lockman.org

Scripture quotations marked NLT are taken from the Holy Bible, New Living Translation. © 1996, 2004, 2015 by Tyndale House Foundation. Used by permission of Tyndale House Publishers, Inc., Carol Stream, Illinois 60188. All rights reserved.

Any internet addresses, phone numbers, or company or product information printed in this book are offered as a resource and are not intended in any way to be or to imply an endorsement by Thomas Nelson, nor does Thomas Nelson vouch for the existence, content, or services of these sites, phone numbers, companies, or products beyond the life of this book.

Library of Congress Cataloging-in-Publication Data

Names: Maher, Brittany, 1991- author. | Speer, Cassandra, 1989- author.
Title: Her true worth: breaking free from a culture of selfies, side hustles, and people pleasing to embrace your true identity in Christ / Brittany Maher and Cassandra Speer, leaders of the her True Worth Community.
Description: Nashville, Tennessee: Nelson Books, [2022] | Includes bibliographical references. | Summary: "Brittany Maher and Cassandra Speer, leaders of the social media sensation and ministry Her True Worth, deliver a powerful call to women to break free from the bondage of false identities and discover their true worth in Jesus Christ"—Provided by publisher.
Identifiers: LCCN 2022003731 (print) | LCCN 2022003732 (ebook) | ISBN 9781400231126 (hc) | ISBN 9781400231157 (epub) | ISBN 9781400231171 (audiobook)
Subjects: LCSH: Christian women—Religious life. | Identity (Psychology)—Religious aspects—Christianity.
Classification: LCC BV4527 .M2355 2022 (print) | LCC BV4527 (ebook) | DDC 248.8/43—dc23/eng/20220223
LC record available at https://lccn.loc.gov/2022003731
LC ebook record available at https://lccn.loc.gov/2022003732

Printed in the United States of America

22 23 24 25 26 LSC 10 9 8 7 6 5 4 3 2 1

For every woman who has ever questioned if she's worthy of the space she takes in this world, these words were written for you. May you develop a deeper understanding of your true worth and identity in Jesus within the pages of this book. You are seen, known, and dearly loved by God. He calls you worthy.

Contents

Contents

Introduction
Who Decides Your Worth?

HAVE YOU EVER LET SOMEONE else's opinion matter more than God's? Or have you allowed something or someone to cause you to question your worth?

A person who doubted you

The number on the scale

Criticism from your boss

An unhealthy relationship

The one who abandoned you

An influencer with the perfect life

The toxic part of side-hustle culture that never stops

An unfollow on social media

The lack of likes on your selfie

Criticism from parents

The supermom who can do it all

The list could go on and on.

If you're like us, you end up looking to others for validation or acceptance; our worth rises and falls on their opinions. What a horrible hamster wheel to run on. It's always a moving target and a never-ending quest for approval.

Am I enough?
Will I ever measure up?
Am I worthy of the space I take in this world?

This can't be how life was intended to be lived. This can't be what God had in mind—us constantly chasing after the next thing. The next trend. The next external pressure for internal validation. The perfect aesthetic on Instagram. The Pinterest-worthy life for all to see.

"Keeping up with the Joneses" has escalated to "keeping up with the Kardashians." We are told we have to look the part and have all the things. Ours is a culture addicted to extremes. Everything has to look like it belongs in a magazine: our homes, our cars, our kids, our lips, and our bodies. Envy is on blast, and we are constantly trying to keep up with one another. If not, somehow, we don't measure up.

And that's a problem. Because when the ever-changing world around us gets to determine our value, we will never land on solid ground. We will always be on a journey without a map. Wandering. Looking for our worth in all the wrong places.

As two women who have struggled on this path, we know the harmful impact of allowing the world to define our value. But we have also seen the freedom that comes when we hold God's opinion higher than anyone else's.

There is a better way. A way to freedom. A way to God's truth.

We have learned how to put a stop to the lies and live free.

For the record, we have not mastered this. There are days when we forget who we are and whose we are. But let's take heart in this: Learning to live from the center of your God-given worth is a marathon, not a sprint. We must take it one day at a time.

We have great days when we wake up and remember who we are in Christ, and we have days when we struggle more than we'd like to admit. When we wander and wander and wander. When our worth is for sale.

But, with God's help, we can live anchored in God's truth. With God's help, we can know who we are and have purpose. With God's help, we can reach our full potential as daughters of the Most High God.

The promise of this book is that you can learn how to live *from* worth rather than *for* worth.

You will learn what healthy validation is and where we cross over to affirmation addiction. You will be able to spot the counterfeit identities that the Enemy deceitfully puts before you. We will show you tips and tactics to guide you back to God after a day, a week, a month, or years of wandering away from God.

You will learn that his arms are always wide open to you and that he desires a deep, close, personal relationship with you.

Again, we're not going to pretend we have this figured out. We're figuring this out alongside you. The truth is, you might never be enough for some people. And the good news is you don't have to be. Who told you that you were worthless? No one gets to decide our value outside of God, and he determined long ago that you were worth dying for. If you have felt less-than, like you don't measure up, or if you feel unstable in your relationship with God, please keep reading.

We may not see you face-to-face right now, but we can assure you that we know the ache within your heart that caused you to pick up this book. We know your longing to be loved and the desire to be seen worthy of the space you take in this world. This longing within your heart was planted there by design by the one who created you.

God's glory is so amazing and beautiful that we can't even fathom it. The heavens declare his glory, and the skies proclaim the work of his hands (Psalm 19:1). We are called to do whatever we do all to his glory (1 Corinthians 10:31). The truth is, even when we strive in our own strength, our best is but filthy rags compared to God's glory (Isaiah 64:6). But what a relief it is to know that our best and worst moments aren't the determining factors of our worth. The pressure to perform is off. *He treasures us. He treasures you.*

If this is true for us, we know deep within the depths of our souls it's true about you too.

If the struggle is real for you, we encourage you to keep reading. If you don't know (or have forgotten) your created value in Christ, please keep reading. If you think you've wandered too far, you are in the right place.

Our prayer is that by the time you finish reading this book, you will no longer be captive to the endless pursuit of worth, validation, and affirmation. Instead, you will be equipped to live life secure in Christ and know without a shadow of a doubt who you are in him.

It's time to learn the truth, hold God's opinion higher than any other, and not let anything matter more than what matters most: *Jesus*.

Ready? Let's go.

One

Misplaced Identity
The War for Your Worth

WE LOVE SUPERHERO MOVIES. THEY are exciting, action-packed, and filled with courage and adventure. Most superhero origin stories reach a pivotal point in the film where the main character finally realizes their full potential when they discover who they truly are—their true identity.

Take, for example, Diana Prince, also known as Wonder Woman. In the story from DC Comics, Diana was a mighty warrior from the society of women known as the Amazons. Diana considered herself to be just like the other Amazons when, really, she was so much more. She wasn't just a strong, beautiful, fearless warrior; she was the daughter of a god. But because she didn't know her true identity, she couldn't step into the power she was born with.

If you don't know you are Wonder Woman, you won't be

Wonder Woman. You can have all the power in the world, but if you don't believe it, you will never walk in it. You won't try to fly, block bullets, or save the world. A similar principle is true for us. If we don't know who we are, we will not walk in our God-given potential. We are born with an identity given to us by God. We are daughters of the Most High God, the Creator of heaven and earth. He is the Alpha and Omega, the King of glory.

With every superhero story, there is a supervillain who is actively working to destroy the world. Wonder Woman's arch-nemesis in the 2017 film *Wonder Woman* is Ares, the god of war, the son of Zeus, and her half brother. Ares is an egotistical, bloodthirsty maniac bent on destroying humanity at any cost. Sound familiar?

Our status as daughters of the King gives us our identity, but it also presents us with our adversary. We're at war for our worth. The devil viciously attempts to rob us of our identity because we pose the greatest threat to him when we know who we are in Christ.

The Enemy is our greatest identity thief. Jesus said of him, "The thief comes only to steal and kill and destroy. I came that they may have life and have it abundantly" (John 10:10 ESV).

The devil has been stealing from the beginning. He will stop at nothing to eradicate what God is doing in us and through us. And most of the time, in our experience, the first place he tries to attack is our identity. Identity is where everything about us begins and is rooted from.

Without identity, we flounder.

Without identity, we are lost.

Without identity, we have nothing grounding us and keeping us firmly rooted and established in who we really are.

Knowing and understanding our true identity is the foundation of everything we do and everything we become. Because without it, we lose our hope—our purpose—and we are easily tossed about by the waves of culture and others' expectations of us.

We need to know our identity in order to carry out the purpose God has for our lives.

One of the subtle ways the Enemy tries to steal our identity is to get us to settle for a "characteristic identity." A characteristic identity is any role or activity to which we attach our value and sense of worth. A characteristic identity might satisfy us for a while, but when that role or activity ends, it takes our identity with it.

We see this happen all the time.

The mom who doesn't know who she is outside of her children.

The businesswoman who loses herself after losing her job.

The athlete who goes through an identity crisis after having an injury and not being able to play her sport anymore.

The straight-A student who hates herself for getting a B in one of her classes.

But what if we could cling to an identity that never changes?

My Identity as Brittany

I'm Brittany: a wife, mother, daughter, sister, aunt, friend, writer, musician, artist, and so much more. Although these identity characteristics are all true of me, none of them are what make me "me." My identity characteristics may be how others view me or how I'm positioned in society, but they aren't who I *am*.

I wasn't born a wife or mother. I didn't come out of my mother's womb singing notes and strumming a guitar or with a paintbrush in my hand. These are simply roles and activities I acquired over time. But my most fundamental identity is that I am uniquely and intentionally formed in the image of God. I am his daughter.

I am fearfully and wonderfully made. That is how God describes me in Scripture (Psalm 139:14). It's who I am. That is the core of my being. Beloved. When I function from that identity, everything beyond that is just an identity characteristic—a role or activity that could end or change without making me lose my identity or undermining who I am in God. But I didn't always know who I was. And sometimes, I still forget.

When I worked as a makeup artist in the beauty industry, I remember how much I loathed wearing a full face of makeup every day. Yet at the same time, I couldn't be without it. I needed makeup on my face. I wasn't me without it. I didn't want people to see what I really looked like underneath.

Where I worked, we were required to have a full face of makeup. We had to be presentable, and we had to show up to work every day looking like we knew what we were doing. Which, in that profession, is totally understandable. I wouldn't want to go to a hairstylist who had a terrible haircut.

But at the end of the day, I couldn't *wait* to get in my bathroom and pick up my makeup remover wipes and erase this image that I felt I needed to maintain at work every day. The makeup

felt greasy on my skin, heavy and uncomfortable. I felt like 1.
identity was quite literally *made up*—a false image of myself to
impress other people. The foundation, eyebrow color, mascara,
eyelashes, lipstick, all of it made up this image I identified with.
I loved and hated it at the same time. I hated having to cake this
stuff on every day, but I was hooked.

I had to suffer through the heaviness from all the product
caked onto my face because I was afraid nobody would know me
without the makeup. They only saw this altered version of me, and
I felt I *had* to keep up with that. I became so used to what I looked
like with the makeup on that when I saw the real, raw version of
myself in the mirror, I didn't recognize the person looking back at
me. I saw her as ugly, plain, and needing enhancement to be beautiful. I didn't feel worthy without makeup. My plain, untouched
face just looked like a blank canvas that was boring and dull.

Don't get me wrong; there isn't anything inherently wrong
with makeup. I know lots of women who can go with or without
it feeling unchanged either way. But for me, it became an identity
problem when I couldn't go without it.

In fact, whenever I begin to wonder if I might be too dependent on something, I ask myself this question: *If God took this
away from me tomorrow, would I be okay?* If the answer is no, it's
possible I've attached my identity to it.

If I lost my makeup bag while I was out of town and needed
to be somewhere where I was going to have to be around people
and there were no nearby makeup stores, who would I be? How
could I show up and just be me without all the enhancement? I
couldn't. They'd hate me.

n I married my husband, Ryan, I was so afraid

up next to me the morning after our wedding

never seen me without my makeup. I remem-

...ing to the bathroom to put on a little eyebrow makeup and concealer just in case he saw what I really looked like and changed his mind. Come to find out, Ryan thinks I look beautiful without makeup, but my mind couldn't hear that.

Again, ask, *If God were to take away the thing I identify with tomorrow, how would it affect me? Would my world fall apart?*

To keep myself aligned with who I am in God's eyes, I ask myself these questions:

What does God say about me?
Are my thoughts lining up with God's Word?
Which thoughts need to be thrown in the trash?

I know I'm not alone in getting distracted, because I'm human, and most people long to understand what their true identity is. This desire may account for the popular trends of people trying to "find themselves" or searching for ways to "feel worthy." The result is that everything we do flows from how we see ourselves or how we want others to perceive us. Unfortunately, when that becomes our only avenue for identity, we're willing to do almost anything to attain and maintain our worth without even realizing that we're like hamsters on a wheel that leads to nowhere.

We crave and obsess to know who we are, and when we don't know who we are, we seek to find out at all costs. On our quest, sometimes we try to satisfy that hunger with things that will always leave us hungry. Whether it's through the vehicle of success, beauty, or intelligence, it's a very human desire to want to feel worthy, loved, important, and seen.

The cross of Christ has already defined our worth from the beginning. God so loved us that he sent his Son to pay the price for our sins so that we could be called sons and daughters of God (John 3:16). We can't earn our status as children of God, or achieve it, or work for it, because our Creator has already determined it through his Son. Isn't that amazing news? The pressure is off because God has already determined our worth and value.

My Identity as Cassandra

I (Cass) have a confession to make. I lived most of my life believing that my presence here on earth held little value. The uncomfortable truth is this: It was easy for me to be convinced that I'm worthless. I perceived the way others treated me, spoke to me, abandoned me, and abused me as solid evidence of my lack of value. I allowed my perception of myself to be determined by the way other people treated me instead of how God created me.

Although I've had the privilege of seeing my family come to Jesus as an adult, I wasn't raised in a Christian household. At a young age I came into agreement with dangerous lies about my identity. I believed my life was an accident, that I was unwanted and hard to love. These lies led me to believe I was worthless. It was a fairly natural conclusion to come to. Only after a great deal of healing and trust in God could I receive the truth that my life has purpose regardless of my circumstances. It wasn't until I was a young adult that I discovered my true worth and identity is and always has been hidden in Christ (Colossians 3:3).

Still, I grew up believing I had to earn my space in this world.

I struggled with the beliefs that my existence was an inconvenience, love was conditional, and my life held very little value. Since early childhood I had the keen awareness that my mother hadn't planned for parenthood, and looking back as a mother of three myself, I have a great deal of compassion for the teenage girl who bravely chose to bring me into this world.

I'm thirty-one years old and twice the age my mother was when she found out she was pregnant with me. Although she didn't plan on motherhood, God always had a plan for my life. The identity of my biological father and the circumstances of my conception remain unknown to me, but from the moment I was conceived, the Enemy was determined to take me out—and he nearly succeed before I even exited my mother's womb.

I spent most of my life wounded and wandering. Like a misshapen puzzle piece that doesn't quite fit, the harder I tried to force myself into spaces I didn't belong, the more tattered and bruised I became.

Have you ever been so desperate to belong that you were willing to forfeit who you were in exchange for acceptance? This is where I slowly raise my hand and admit I have. Numerous times.

I relied on popular opinion to assess my worth. I didn't discuss my thoughts or share my feelings out of fear of rejection. I lived under the false banner that it's better to be seen and not heard. I also believed the lie that I needed to be compliant and accommodating in order to be loved. I used to skid through life with surface-level friendships. I know now that I battle a deep-seated fear that if I were ever to truly allow someone to know me, they'd realize I wasn't worthy of their love, and they'd leave me.

This fear is the rotten fruit produced through experiencing abandonment. In an attempt to avoid the sting of rejection, I tried to become someone else. Anyone else. Someone I thought might be worthy of love because, in my mind, I wasn't. I went through phases like all teenagers do. I blended in, behaved like the girls I wanted to be accepted by, and eventually achieved what I thought was the ultimate goal—attention and popularity.

Dear friend, popularity at the cost of your identity is a cheap trade. Don't buy into it.

Through Christ and his sacrifice on the cross, my life has immeasurable value. My trust in Jesus changed my life and re-defined my family tree. The statistics stacked up against me were abolished. The curses that plagued generations before me no longer held authority. What was once a generational cycle ended with me.

To look upon our lives and believe we're created with inherent value requires faith—because, more often than not, the world has a thousand reasons we shouldn't believe this to be true. Thankfully, we can look throughout the Bible and see that God defines worth and value differently than the world. Scripture says, "We have this treasure in jars of clay to show that this all-surpassing power is from God and not from us" (2 Corinthians 4:7).

Did you know that these jars of clay were essentially made of mud? Often what people might consider worthless, God deems exquisite. I find it extraordinary that God made Adam from the dust of the ground (Genesis 2:7), and he placed his most valuable treasure within a vessel formed of the very same dirt and mud. The cross says everything you and I need to know about our worth and value to God. Why would Jesus die on a cross if we weren't worth anything? Who pays such a high, life-giving price for something of no value? Would you go to the grocery store and pay a hundred dollars for a pack of gum? Of course not! Likewise, God wouldn't send his one and only Son to die for the price of your salvation if you didn't mean something significant to him in the first place. "God shows his love for us in that while we were still sinners, Christ died for us" (Romans 5:8 esv).

My favorite part of this verse is that it says "while we were still sinners." In other words, we cannot earn grace or achieve our worthiness when it comes to God. The truth is, we aren't inherently worthy on our own. If we were, we would have no need for Christ. We aren't worthy of his grace, but he sent his Son anyway.

While we were still sinners, God sent his Son.

While we were still sinners, Jesus died for us.

Not everything you read in the Bible is about you, but everything in the Bible was written to point you to God. The universe doesn't revolve around you, but the same hands that created the heavens and the earth carefully formed you.

You were created in God's image, and your life is for his glory. And yes, even your weaknesses point to his strength, your wounds point to his ability to heal, and the ruins of your life point to his power to restore and redeem. That's because humanity is different from the rest of God's beautiful creation; we alone bear the image of the Creator.

God said, "Let us make mankind in our image, in our likeness, so that they may rule over the fish in the sea and the birds in the sky, over the livestock and all the wild animals, and over all the creatures that move along the ground."

So God created mankind in his own image,
in the image of God he created them;
male and female he created them.

(GENESIS 1:26–27)

Notice this verse doesn't say that God created trees in his image or birds in his image. God intentionally designed human beings—you and me—in his image and in his likeness.

What does it mean to be formed in the image of God? It means that God created us with inherent value, each possessing our own unique personalities, feelings, and free will. This sets us apart from the rest of creation. To be an image bearer of God means that we reflect our Creator. Not in physical attributes, such as hands and feet, but in his character. As image bearers of God, we are to reflect his heart, his attributes, his personhood.

The most accurate description of God is found in his Word. The apostle John wrote, "Dear friends, let us love one another, for love comes from God. Everyone who loves has been born of

God and knows God. Whoever does not love does not know God, because God is love" (1 John 4:7–8).

John made it clear that God is love. Let's take it a step further and look at the biblical definition of love penned by the apostle Paul:

> Love is patient, love is kind. It does not envy, it does not boast, it is not proud. It does not dishonor others, it is not self-seeking, it is not easily angered, it keeps no record of wrongs. Love does not delight in evil but rejoices with the truth. It always protects, always trusts, always hopes, always perseveres.
>
> Love never fails. (1 Corinthians 13:4–8)

You see, we were meant to reflect God's image, which is love. We do that when our lives reflect the characteristics Paul described.

We Reflect God's Image

I (Britt) got a unique glimpse into how amazing it is to be made in the image of God when my husband, Ryan, and I had our first child, Ariana. She's such a little squish! I love her so much.

The first time I looked down at her precious face, I couldn't stop gazing at all her physical attributes to see how she resembled both my husband and me. It was truly amazing to look at this tiny miracle and know that she was made from both of us. Yet I find so much comfort in knowing that not only is she made in our image, but she is also created in the image of God. God himself fearfully and wonderfully made my daughter. It's so surreal. He knitted her life together in my womb (Psalm 139:13–14).

Just as there is so much more to Ariana than the physical attributes she got from her parents, there is so much more to you and me than the genetic makeup we received from our parents. We are uniquely, purposefully designed by our Creator and made to reflect his image and likeness. How amazing is that?

To know who we truly are in him and how to reflect his image, we need to know who he is by spending time with him and reading his Word. This points us to the truth that we were created to live in communion with God, to live with our lives, bodies, and souls fully exposed and without shame in God's presence. God's original design was for us to have intimacy with him. Sadly, that intimacy was shattered when sin entered the world.

How the Devil Schemes to Hide Our Identity from Us

In the garden of Eden, God placed a loving boundary on Adam and Eve.

> You must not eat from the tree of the knowledge of good and evil, for when you eat from it you will certainly die. (Genesis 2:17)

Instead of challenging the boundary directly, notice how Satan challenged God when he tempted Eve.

> He said to the woman, "Did God really say, 'You must not eat from any tree in the garden'?"
>
> The woman said to the serpent, "We may eat fruit from the trees in the garden, but God did say, 'You must not eat fruit from the tree that is in the middle of the garden, and you must not touch it, or you will die.'"
>
> "You will not certainly die," the serpent said to the woman. "For God knows that when you eat from it your eyes will be opened, and you will be like God, knowing good and evil." (Genesis 3:1–5)

This tactic of challenging God is one the Enemy continues to use because, unfortunately, it's still so effective. If he can get us to question God, the battle is half won. Why? Because if the Enemy can cause us to second-guess what we know to be true, we're more easily manipulated.

The Enemy likes to distract us and distort the truth, but even an attractive misdirection is a lie. And we all know what happened when Adam and Eve fell for the lie.

> When the woman saw that the fruit of the tree was good for food and pleasing to the eye, and also desirable for gaining wisdom, she took some and ate it. She also gave some to her husband, who was with her, and he ate it. Then the eyes of both of them were opened, and they realized they were naked;

so they sewed fig leaves together and made coverings for themselves. (Genesis 3:6–7)

Adam and Eve immediately tried to cover themselves when sin entered the world, leaving them suddenly exposed, aware and insecure about their nakedness. In an instant, what God had called good became shameful. Their instinct to hide was an outward expression of their internal response to guilt and shame.

Something similar happens when we feel guilt and shame over wrongdoing. The voice of condemnation whispers, "You'd better cover up this struggle." While the voice of conviction from the Holy Spirit of God says, "Come close. Let's expose this sin and strip shame of its grip on you."

For example, if you fall into the sin of gossip, the voice of condemnation says, "There you go gossiping again. You'll never be free from this. People won't trust you either." But the voice of godly conviction says, "I'd better go to my Father and ask for his help and his strength to put off this sin of gossip in my life."

The truth is, the Enemy wants you to live in doubt, tangled up in shame. He wants you to stay hidden from God, afraid to expose yourself or what you've done.

If we stay hidden, we're living in isolation, which is a breeding ground for sin and shame. But we can never truly be hidden from God. There's nowhere we can go that his loving gaze cannot reach us.

The apostle Paul wrote, "There is now no condemnation for those who are in Christ Jesus, because through Christ Jesus the law of the Spirit who gives life has set you free from the law of sin and death" (Romans 8:1–2).

We were made to carry the image of God. Sin separated us from that image. But that doesn't mean God can't come in and restore what has been lost. Again, Satan will use misdirection, temptation, and manipulation to keep us separated from our true identity in Christ. Our lives are hidden in him (Colossians 3:3).

In Christ, the lost are found, the broken are redeemed, and what the Enemy tries to abolish, Jesus comes to redeem and restore.

Beloved, you're not too dirty or too broken for the healing and redemptive love that is found in God through Christ Jesus. No matter what you've done or what's been done to you, there's no sin that can separate you from the loving God who created you.

Even when you feel like you've lost yourself, God has never lost sight of you.

Reflect and Respond

1. Have you clung to something in your life so tightly that if God were to take it away, it would devastate you? If so, write the first thing that comes to mind.
2. Do you have a friend who seems totally secure in their identity in Christ? How has their friendship influenced your life in a positive way?

3. How does it make you feel to know you were created in God's image?

4. When was the first time you questioned your worth? How did that experience affect your life?

Two

People Pleasing
The Lies We Believe

I WANT TO TELL YOU the lies I (Britt) believed for years—and still find myself believing at times.

Sadly, these lies all started in my childhood when my parents were going through a messy divorce. Isn't it funny that the Enemy can get us believing the lies he tells us from such a young, innocent, impressionable age?

Even though my parents are both great people and I love them dearly, I was just seven years old when they divorced. My two older brothers and I were caught in the middle of their feuds. It was painful to be pawns in their battles against each other. (Spoiler: I've since become an adult and realize that my wonderful parents make mistakes, just like I do.)

As you can imagine, as a then seven-year-old little girl, the only time I ever felt worthy or enough was when I was entertaining one of my parents or family members by being a listening ear to their hurt feelings or gossip about my other parent or family members.

"Your mom did this and said that."

"Your dad did this and said that."

I felt like I had to choose which parent or family I loved more instead of just being loved by them and feeling secure in my role as their child.

Back then I'm sure it didn't seem like a big deal to them to argue in front of us, but to me it felt like more and more of my childhood was being chewed up and spit out. Naturally, I hated that my parents were no longer together, and it hurt every time someone mentioned it, which was often.

All this laid the groundwork for me to become a people pleaser. And people pleasing comes from feeling worthy only when everybody is happy and pleased with you. What a lie and trick from the devil!

I'm worthy only if everyone is happy with me. Gosh! That shaped me for so long. It trickled into adulthood and into every relationship I've ever been in. I was only as good as my next pat on the back, my next "I love you," or my next "You make me so happy."

Starting young, my identity was wrapped up in pleasing the people around me—and that was exacerbated by the cruel social world of middle schoolers.

When I was in middle school, I would see all the skinny and popular girls getting attention from all the cute boys. Even the teachers loved them. I remember one day in gym class, a pretty and popular girl came up to me for no reason at all and told me that I was fat and looked like a boy. Then she went on to laugh about it with a group of other girls. I stood there, embarrassed and questioning my self-worth at twelve years old. It felt like a scene straight from the movie *Mean Girls*. It was then that I began believing the lie that unless I was beautiful and skinny, I wasn't ever going to be truly loved and accepted. Why did I suddenly desire their approval? What puzzle piece was missing in me that I needed fulfillment and affirmation from people I didn't even know?

Those years set me on a long path of battling with body-image issues and eating disorders well into my young adult life. From anorexia and body dysmorphia to extreme binge eating and bulimia, I've believed the lies that my worthiness and being loved depend on me making my body pleasing to others and keeping those around me happy.

I'd like to say that all my efforts at people pleasing ended after adolescence, but I still struggle sometimes—especially when it comes to social media.

A few years back I was at a social event where lots of pictures were being taken.

"Brittany! Come take a picture with us!" Boom—immediate anxiety knowing the photos would be posted on social media without me being able to "tweak" them first.

Even if it was just a selfie, I believed that my real and authentic self simply wasn't good enough. I had to look perfect, and perfection was so easily attainable with a filter adjustment. With just a quick toggle of a bar, I could whiten my teeth, slim my face, slim my body, make my eyelashes longer and thicker. You name it, I did it.

The voice in my head went something like this:

If I look perfect, they'll love me. I'll be desired. If I just tweak this image a little bit, then they'll hit the Like button and prove to me and to the rest of the world that I'm important and loved. People will envy me and my perfect life . . . even though I actually feel empty inside.

Anyone relate?

Cass's Story

Although Britt and I grew up in very different households, our stories echo with similarities. I also grew up believing I had to earn my space in this world. Like Britt, I allowed countless lies about my appearance to define me throughout my life, even in my career as a hairstylist. I spent most of my life battling disordered eating and white-knuckling to keep a semblance of control. Things took a turn for the worse when, at age sixteen, I moved with my family from Wisconsin to a small city in Texas with borders that stretched across not one but two states. I was nestled deep within the Bible Belt, a term I'd never heard until my arrival.

So there I was, a bleach-blonde northern girl living in a

sweet-tea-sippin' small-town world. Culture shock doesn't even begin to cover it.

Looking back, it's comical how disoriented I was. I went from living in a non-Christian home to living in a town where there was a church on every corner. Often across the street from each other. The first time I saw a man in Walmart wearing Wrangler jeans, boots, and a big Texas belt buckle, I nudged my mom and said, "Look. It's a cowman! A real live cowman." As if he were some mythical creature that only existed in old Western films. My mother's quick response was "Hush. It's a cowboy, and don't point."

The first day of school was just as awkward. I was 100 percent prepared to carry my lunch tray into the burnt-orange bathroom and eat my stale chicken nuggets alone in a stall, but of course that didn't happen. A girl with a charming twang gestured to me from a table full of complete strangers across the cafeteria. Apparently, word had gotten out that there was a new girl in town because every single person at that lunch table knew my name, and I hadn't introduced myself to a soul. (If you're from a small town, you don't need me to tell you that news spreads fast! The good, the bad, and the risqué. It all gets passed around like your favorite dish at a Southern Baptist potluck.)

Slightly horrified and heart racing, I plopped my cheeks in a seat, surrounded by strangers with all eyes on me. I had moved from a school where my graduating class had more kids than my new school's entire population. Talk about a fish out of water! I would be flopping around and floundering to find "my people" long after graduation day.

By the time I entered eleventh grade, I was given the option of taking cosmetology classes. Because I'd transferred from out of state, my credits didn't line up. They didn't know what to do with me, so they offered me two options: take college courses or trade school half a day twice a week. I chose playing with hair and makeup, obviously. I completed my license in cosmetology within months of graduating from high school. At eighteen years old, barely a woman but no longer a little girl, I moved out. Desperate to escape what was at the time a difficult home environment, I needed to get out on my own. With limited resources, the beauty industry was my ticket out.

I'll never forget my first salon and spa job. Y'all, I thought I had arrived. I began as an apprentice at a swanky salon in our small town in Texas. It was painfully evident that I didn't belong there, but boy, did I want to. The owners also owned an upscale boutique attached to the salon that carried a very limited variety of sizes and gorgeous name-brand clothing that far exceeded my budget.

All the girls at the salon and spa were expected to wear the clothing they sold in the boutique. The owners generously offered a steep employee discount that made that type of luxury possible. They also paid for all their employees to have memberships at the highest-quality health and wellness gym our city had to offer. Only one not-so-small issue. I couldn't fit my Texas-sized bottom into those bougie, bedazzled blue jeans. So I did what I thought I had to do. If my body refused to fit into the clothes in the boutique, I'd alter my body and starve it into submission.

Listen, friend. I hope this goes without saying, but,

unfortunately, I had to learn this the hard way: clothes are made to fit you; you weren't created to fit the clothes.

In my eyes, my size was a problem to be solved and yet another painful reminder that I didn't deserve to be there. Even worse, I continued to buy into the lie that said I needed to earn my place in that space. I worked tirelessly to lose weight, resorting to unhealthy diets and extreme exercise habits to achieve the goal. No cost was too high. There wasn't a line I wouldn't cross. I binged and I purged. I even convinced a doctor to write me a weight-loss prescription that made my heart pound out of my chest.

I would tell myself that it was my responsibility to fit into the mold they had chosen for me. They were paying for my gym membership after all! *I'm lucky to be here*, I'd tell myself. *I'm grateful to be here, and I need to prove that I deserve to be here.* I slowly lost myself in the pursuit of belonging to that world. I worked in a toxic environment where they broke you down in order to build you back up into their image.

I used to have nightmares about the piercing sound of the owner's high heels against the hard concrete pavement. *Click, clack, clickity-clack, clack.* If that wasn't a clear indication I needed to get out of there quickly, I don't know what was—but I refused to quit. I couldn't give up. I felt I needed that job to feel valuable. I endured the insults and suffering in order to feel worthwhile.

The memory of my last day at what I thought was my dream job is forever etched in my heart and mind. I had back-to-back clients from the moment I arrived. I was toggling back and forth between the salon and the spa.

12:30 p.m.: Allover color and style
2:00 p.m.: Brow tint and lip wax
2:30 p.m.: Haircut and style
3:30 p.m.: Basic manicure and pedicure
5:00 p.m.: Spa pedicure

After I'd finished with my last client at the end of an exhausting day, I thought I was the only employee left in the salon until I noticed a large black trash bag at my workstation. *Hmm, that's weird*, I thought. I barely had the opportunity to finish that thought before I heard the loud *click, clack, clickity-clack, clack* of my boss's high heels quickly approaching behind me.

"Cass, we need to talk. Follow me to my office," my boss said.

With a deep sense of impending doom, I followed.

When we got there, she asked me to sit down and proceeded to inform me that she was letting me go. She had thrown all my tools and belongings into the large trash bag on my station earlier that day.

I was crushed and humiliated when I realized that all my belongings were in that humongous trash bag for everyone to see long before she shared the news with me.

"Well, the problem is that when you're good, you're fantastic, and when you're not, you're horrible. Can you explain to me why my granddaughter who's in kindergarten can give a basic manicure better than you?" she asked.

Her words shook me to my core. I paused before I opened my mouth. I was hired to work in the salon as a hairstylist and never presented myself as a nail technician, but I had never challenged her authority or so much as disagreed with her up to this point. I deeply considered my next words and replied, "Would anything I have to say in response to your question change the fact that I no longer have a job here?"

"No," she said.

"Then I see no reason to continue this conversation further," I shakily replied.

She silently nodded her head, handed me my cash tips for the day, and escorted me to collect my things. There it was again. The Hefty trash bag sitting on my station. I saw a glimpse of my reflection in the mirror when I grabbed hold of the drawstring. *This is who I am, and this is what I've always been*, I thought to myself. In that terrible moment, it seemed like all my worst fears had been confirmed. I was worthless—just like the trash bag I carried in my hand.

Looking back, I can clearly see how the lies I believed led me to place my worth in my appearance, define myself by my career, and ultimately take on a counterfeit identity.

How Do I Know If I've Taken on a Counterfeit Identity?

You might be asking, How do I know whether I've developed a counterfeit identity?

To help answer that question, let's identify the worldly tools we tend to use to measure our worth:

- work
- weight
- how people perceive you
- money
- popularity
- success
- achievements
- relationships
- appearance
- material things
- likes on social media
- followers
- being desired

The list goes on and on.

It's true that we can get quick identity boosters from the world. Sure, they make us feel good for a little while. They're like a credit card with a high interest rate: they require minimal investment on the front end, but over time the charges add up, and the interest on the balance continues to increase. If we live life attaching our identity to these cheap counterfeits, when the bill comes due, we'll never have enough to pay. We'll be indentured servants to the very things we thought were serving us. It turns out those same things take from us more than they actually give. But the Enemy doesn't want us to know this truth. If he can keep us chasing after the world's measures of worth and value, we'll never truly be free.

Thankfully, our true worth and value is found in Christ, and through him our debt is paid in full.

> He chose us in him before the creation of the world to be holy and blameless in his sight. In love he predestined us for adoption to sonship through Jesus Christ, in accordance with his pleasure and will—to the praise of his glorious grace, which he has freely given us in the One he loves. In him we have redemption through his blood, the forgiveness of sins, in accordance with the riches of God's grace that he lavished on us. With all wisdom and understanding, he made known to us the mystery of his will according to his good pleasure, which he purposed in Christ, to be put into effect when the times reach their fulfillment—to bring unity to all things in heaven and on earth under Christ. (Ephesians 1:4–10)

Remember that question I (Britt) said I ask myself to see if I've misplaced my identity? Ask yourself, *If God were to take away this thing I identify with tomorrow, how would it affect me? Would I be okay?* If the answer is no, you've allowed that measurement of worth to become an idol in your life, and it's a counterfeit identity you need to shed.

So if we are giving our worship to things like success or relationships, the moment we don't have those things we go through an identity crisis.

When you use the world's tools to assess your worth, your

measurements will always be off. You'll find yourself trying to measure up against something that will always leave you feeling like you've fallen short. Just as you can't measure something with a hammer or pound nails with a measuring tape, you can't use worldly tools to measure your value and worth. You were never meant to use those tools.

The cross is the ultimate measure of your worth and value. *Jesus* is the only measuring tool that matters. So now you can ditch all the other wrong tools and rest in the truth that the finished work of Christ on the cross is what determines your true worth and value. When you grasp that truth, that's when you will feel complete in who you are. We must replace lies with the truth of God's Word.

Replacing Lies with Truth

Did you know that Jesus described Satan as the "father of lies"? Here's what Jesus said:

> [The devil] was a murderer from the beginning, not holding to the truth, for there is no truth in him. When he lies, he speaks his native language, for he is a liar and the father of lies. (John 8:44)

Did you catch that part about lies being Satan's native tongue? In other words, he is incapable of speaking anything but a lie. Now that you know this, we implore you to never fall for the lies again. Anytime you hear his lies, know that God is saying the exact opposite.

Jesus = *Truth*
Satan = *Lies*

There is *no* truth in Satan. We desire to help you dismantle and break every single lie and stronghold in your life so you can find freedom in Christ and know exactly who you are in him. To do that, you must confront lies by speaking truth to them and over yourself. This is how we as daughters of God allow the Holy Spirit to make that our reality. The apostle Paul put it this way: "We demolish arguments and every pretension that sets itself up against the knowledge of God, and we take captive every thought to make it obedient to Christ" (2 Corinthians 10:5). This includes the lies we've been taught, both indirectly and intentionally.

We're going to tackle false beliefs we've held as gospel truth, and we're going to dispel the lies that have held our hearts hostage for far too long. Here are some examples of what it looks like to replace lies with truth.

LIES	TRUTH
You are hopeless.	You are alive with Christ. (Ephesians 2:5)
You are alone.	You are seen by God. (Genesis 16:13-14) God places the lonely in families. (Psalm 68:6)

You're not good enough, and you never will be.	You are the righteousness of God in Christ Jesus. (2 Corinthians 5:21)
You are worthless.	You are treasured by God. (2 Corinthians 4:7)
You are weak.	Greater is he who is in you than he who is in the world. (1 John 4:4)
You can't to do anything right.	You are greatly loved by God. (Romans 1:7; Ephesians 2:4; Colossians 3:12)
Your life isn't important.	You can do all things through Christ Jesus. (Philippians 4:13)
You'll never find healing.	By his wounds you are healed. (Isaiah 53:5)
You won't get through hard things.	You are more than a conqueror through him who loves you. (Romans 8:37)
Your past defines you.	You are a new creation in Christ. (2 Corinthians 5:17)

We want to take a moment to acknowledge that lies aren't just things we think; they are things we act on and are wounded by.

Here's how a lie I (Britt) believed unfolded in my life:

Lie: I'm worthless because I'm overweight.

How I act on the lie: I starve myself and abuse my body.

How it affects my life: I obsess over my appearance and hide from people because I am so embarrassed about the way I look.

The wound it leaves: I loathe the body God gave me.

Now reread my list from bottom to top.

See how a lie that leads to a wound can become a tox. It's what the Enemy wants. Okay, now let me show you how the truth of Christ met me in that single lie:

> *Truth:* I'm exactly who God made me to be, stretch marks and all. I am fearfully and wonderfully made. (Psalm 139:13–14)
>
> *How I act on the truth:* I take care of my body and glorify God with it. The Holy Spirit dwells within me. I honor God by intentionally caring for my body. (1 Corinthians 6:19–20)
>
> *How it affects my life:* I am free from the weight of others' opinions and from the weight on the scale. My value is no longer tethered to these things. My true worth and identity are found in Christ. (Colossians 3:3)
>
> *The healing I experience:* I love my body and am thankful for it every day. What a difference the truth makes!

We call this process of replacing lies with truth the "freedom framework." You can use the same process to help you identify the lies in your life and replace them with truth.

Lie: _____.

How I act on the lie: _____.

How it affects my life: _____.

The wound it leaves: _____.

Truth: _____.

How I can act on the truth: _____.

How it will affect my life: _____.

The healing I want to experience through

    Christ:_____.

Our prayer is that the freedom framework above helps you break free from any toxic loop you may be stuck in. The Enemy wants us trapped in a hamster wheel of lies, but thanks be to God that he provides freedom.

We just walked you through how to replace lies with truth. Now we want to address the wounds those lies leave behind and why it's important to swiftly deal with the pain these lies inflict.

Rip Off the Band-Aid, Sis

We're not sure what you've been told, but the weary and the wounded are always welcome at the feet of Jesus.

> Come to me, all you who are weary and burdened, and I will give you rest. Take my yoke upon you and learn from me, for I am gentle and humble in heart, and you will find rest for your souls. For my yoke is easy and my burden is light. (Matthew 11:28–30)

We often avoid dealing with the wounds that come from lies. Here are few reasons we might avoid tackling these wounds:

- We're afraid of confronting the lie.
- We might believe it's easier to ignore the lie.
- We've lived so long believing the lie that we no longer recognize that we've fallen victim to it.

Choosing to avoid these wounds will only deepen our pain and tighten the grasp they have on us. Who better to trust with the contents of your heart than the one who created it?! The wound you refuse to address likely holds the healing your soul desperately needs to access. Bring your pain to Jesus, friend.

It's never easy or enjoyable to talk about the lies we believe and the wounds we carry, but to promote healing we must first find where we need to be healed. We know that believing a lie for years and years can continue to deepen wounds that we have. Sometimes when we don't even realize it, those wounds can alter the way we perceive ourselves, others, and situations in our lives.

Imagine having a large cut on your right arm. This cut has bruising around it. It's bleeding and infected, and it hurts your entire arm. You obviously aren't going to use that arm because it's incapable of being used. You're also most likely going to move very gingerly with it and make sure not to bump it because you could hurt it worse.

Like a *physical* wound, an *emotional* wound can incapacitate us. For instance, if someone you've put all your trust and loyalty in betrays you in some grand way, you're probably going to have a hard time trusting people. And when the next person comes along, you might keep your guard up because of what happened to you before. You're going to be very guarded with your heart to make sure you don't get hurt again.

One of These Things Is Not Like the Other

It's easy to give in to the temptation to assign our worth and value to external things. Do you remember what Jesus said about how to distinguish true prophets from counterfeit prophets?

> You'll know them by their . . . fancy houses and cars? No.
> You'll know them by their . . . Instagram followers? No.
> You'll know them by their . . . impressive jobs? No.
> You'll know them by their . . . nice bodies? No.
> You'll know them by their *fruit*? Yes. (Matthew 7:15–20)

We're the first to admit counterfeits are appealing. Who doesn't like the way it feels to have what the world considers success and happiness? The trouble with this concept is that the world and the Word are often at odds with each other. Wait, wait, wait. Are we saying that worldly success is evil? No, of course not. But we are saying that striving to achieve what the world considers success is a fruitless ambition. Have that side hustle, but have it in a healthy way.

Producing good fruit in our lives requires discipline and a lifelong commitment. The Enemy knows this and likes to draw us in with quick fixes and half-truths. Jesus warns us, "Enter through the narrow gate. For wide is the gate and broad is the road that leads to destruction, and many enter through it. But small is the gate and narrow the road that leads to life, and only a few find it" (Matthew 7:13–14).

Sometimes when we take on a counterfeit identity, it's not always as apparent as we think. That's why it's so important to saturate ourselves in the Word of God—so we can use his Word to measure our hearts and see where we need his transforming love to come and clean house.

In our attempt to find our worth, we attach it to things that don't promise us eternal freedom. A counterfeit identity might look good for all the world to see, but it will never set you free.

I (Britt) have known people in my life who had all the things the world considers markers of value and worth, but, at the end of the day, they still didn't know who they were. It is possible to have all the things but at the cost of true freedom. Because just when you think you have it all, there will always be more things you need to shore up your value.

Having all the things, having the best body, the best car, the best house, the best clothes, the best job, the most success—none of it can compare to the true freedom found in Christ. It's an endless pursuit to try to find validation in anything but Christ.

It's like having a bowl of fake fruit on your table. When you have guests come in, they see the shiny fruit, but it's only to see, not to consume. Artificial fruit looks good enough to eat but it's plastic to the core. You can't offer any real sustenance with the fake fruit.

Speaking of fruit, we love what Jesus taught about how to distinguish the real thing from the counterfeit.

Watch out for false prophets. They come to you in sheep's clothing, but inwardly they are ferocious wolves. By their fruit you will recognize them. Do people pick grapes from thornbushes, or figs from thistles? Likewise, every good tree bears good fruit, but a bad tree bears bad fruit. A good tree cannot bear bad fruit, and a bad tree cannot bear good fruit. Every tree that does not bear good fruit is cut down and thrown into the fire. Thus, by their fruit you will recognize them. (Matthew 7:15–20)

Jesus' point was that not everything is as it seems. To distinguish the sheep from the wolves in our lives, we need to look beyond appearances to the fruit—to what is produced. Although we may not routinely need to distinguish between true and false prophets in our everyday lives, we do need to distinguish between the true and false messages we consume—especially when those messages influence our identity. We need to ask questions like these:

- Who am I listening to?
- What do they value?
- What are they teaching me?
- What is the fruit of their life or message?
- Is this person or message creating good fruit or bad fruit in my life?

These are important questions to consider when examining the voices you allow to speak into your life. False messages are everywhere, and they sow seeds of discontentment and discord wherever they go.

Consuming fake fruit will always leave us starving for real sustenance. Our experiences and feelings are not our identity. Why do we let someone or something other than Jesus determine who we are?

Let's not allow the lies of the Enemy and the messages of a misguided culture carry more weight than what God has said about our identity, value, and purpose.

Refuse the plastic, shiny fruit, and pursue Jesus.

Refuse the counterfeits, sister.

Reflect and Respond

1. What do you think of when you hear the word *identity*? How would you describe yourself?
2. Are you a people pleaser? How has the pursuit of gaining the approval of people affected your life?
3. How does it make you feel to be told you can't earn God's love?
4. Have you ever allowed a lie to anchor itself within your heart? If so, take a moment to tackle the lie with the freedom framework.

Three

Affirmation Addiction

*Chasing After Our Worth
in All the Wrong Places*

HELLO, OUR NAMES ARE BRITT and Cass, and we're affirmation addicts.

You might be wondering, *What is affirmation, and how does it apply to me?* Well, we're so glad you asked! Let's begin with defining the term.

Affirm: (verb)

1. state as a fact; assert strongly and publicly
2. declare one's support for; uphold; defend
3. accept or confirm the validity of (a judgment or agreement); ratify
4. offer someone emotional support or encouragement[1]

We love to be affirmed in all these ways. What could be better than having someone say nice things about us publicly, declare their support for us, agree with us, and offer us support and encouragement?

Affirmation from others makes all of us feel accepted, supported, and validated. When people send affirmation our way, it makes us feel we are on the right path in life. After all, we all want acceptance and love, right? Our longing for affirmation is a God-given desire that lies deep within the heart of each and every one of us. Children look for affirmation from their parents, whether it's the crayon masterpiece ready to be featured on the fridge or advice about a relationship later in life. Students often look for the approval of their teachers on their assignments, and many of us look to each other for solidarity and support.

We all need healthy, godly affirmation. It helps build our self-esteem. Knowing that someone believes in us can help us keep pushing onward when life gets tough.

Given that affirmation is a good thing we all need, what can go wrong with needing it or even being addicted to it? When does the desire for affirmation become unhealthy or even an addiction—something that leads to life-impairing consequences rather than life-enhancing outcomes? The answer to these questions lies within the motivation behind our desire for affirmation and the lengths we're willing to go to acquire it. When we determine our value based on the shifting approval of others instead of the steadfast love of God, we're likely to become dedicated to the pursuit of it.

You might be asking, "How do I know if I'm addicted to affirmation?"

Answer: If every statement about you ends in a question, you might be an affirmation addict. For example:

I'm enough, right?
I'm loved, right?
I'm important, right?
I'm valued, right?
I'm seen and heard, right?

When you feel like you need to be affirmed in order to survive, and to be rejected is to die, you might be addicted to affirmation.

Similarly, when you begin to develop an unhealthy dependency on seeking validation that only God can provide, you might be addicted to affirmation—looking for your worth in all the wrong places. Take a moment to evaluate your heart.

We want you to respond with what you know to be true about yourself, not what you hope to be true. Pause to consider the answers to these questions without judgment or criticism:

If you went about your entire day with people hurling insults at you, would it change how you feel about yourself or how God sees you?

I know this is extreme, but really challenge yourself to think about that.

And the second question:

Does your view of your worth and identity shift when others' opinions change?

If you answered yes to either of these questions, there's a good chance you're entangled in a cycle of affirmation addiction.

If any of that resonates with you, we're here to help you, friend. Consider this your very own affirmation-addiction rehab and break free from needing validation from everyone but God.

How Affirmation Was Twisted into Worship

Story time. Once upon a time, God created a beautiful, powerful, and awesome being—an angel. This angel was full of wisdom, light, and beauty. His name literally meant "light-bearer, shining one, morning star."[2] This guy was impressive and a pretty big deal. He was a top archangel with authority and influence among God's heavenly hosts. This individual had been given everything. He'd been ordained with honor, privilege, and splendor. Some would say that God broke the mold when he was created.

He was the model of perfection and so beautiful that it started to go to his head. He became filled with pride. Perhaps he thought something along these lines:

So, I'm kind of a big deal. Why is God getting all the glory and attention? I'm pretty great too. I'm beautiful. I'm powerful. I'm basically like the Almighty. If anything, he is barely better than me. I deserve some worship too.

By now, you may have inferred that the one we are referring to is Lucifer, a.k.a. Satan, which means the "adversary," the deceiver, and the devil, which means "false accuser" or "slanderer."[3]

Lucifer became so caught up in his own glory that his heart became proud. One minute he was worshipping at the throne of God. The next minute he had made plans to set up his own throne.

A compelling passage of Scripture written by the prophet Isaiah reveals how prideful Lucifer was. Although the passage was originally addressed to the king of Babylon, scholars agree that it also undoubtedly points to Satan.

How you have fallen from heaven,
morning star, son of the dawn!
You have been cast down to the earth,
you who once laid low the nations!
You said in your heart,
"*I will* ascend to the heavens;
I will raise my throne
above the stars of God;
I will sit enthroned on the mount of assembly,
on the utmost heights of Mount Zaphon.
I will ascend above the tops of the clouds;
I will make myself like the Most High."

(ISAIAH 14:12–14, EMPHASIS ADDED)

Notice the five "I will" statements Lucifer made. These statements clearly demonstrate Satan's pride and desire to be worshipped.

God said to Lucifer, "Your heart became proud on account of your beauty, and you corrupted your wisdom because of your splendor" (Ezekiel 28:17).

Have you ever met someone who was really good-looking and knew it? Someone who thought that they were hot stuff because they were, but yet that made them less attractive? Now, times that by a trillion and you have Lucifer.

Lucifer didn't earn the beauty and wisdom that was given to him, yet he decided in his head that he was entitled to be worshipped. First of all, where did he get off thinking he was entitled to anything when everything was given to him? Who would do such a thing?

We would.

Ouch. I know that stings a little bit, but hear us out. Our legitimate desire for affirmation can become twisted into a misguided desire for praise and worship if we're not careful.

The Enemy wants to replicate his mindset in us. In his pride, he wants all the praise and worship for himself, but that's not enough. He wants us to want it too. As a matter of fact, Satan not only wants us to desire to become the focus of others' adoration, but in doing so we also become increasingly desperate for it. Our appetite for affirmation becomes insatiable. We find ourselves addicted to the praise and hooked on the hype.

You might be thinking, *I don't want people to worship me!* At least, that was our initial reaction. But if we're honest, we do want people to praise us. And even though *worship* might be a strong word for it, we really like it when people love us. Those are hard things to admit. And yet we know we have to admit them. If we don't admit them, God can't correct them.

To better understand what it means that the Enemy wants us to have his mindset about praise and worship, let's consider the definitions of both words.

> *Praise:* The expression of warm approval or admiration
> *Worship:* The feeling or expression of reverence and
>   adoration[4]

Now let's take a closer look at the four italicized words in those definitions.

> *Approval:* The belief that someone or something is *good* or
>   *acceptable*
> *Admiration:* *Respect* and warm *approval*
> *Reverence:* Deep *respect* for someone or something
> *Adoration:* Deep *love* and *respect*[5]

Okay, so right off the bat, I have to admit that I want most of these things. I want people to

- approve of me;
- admire me;
- have reverence for me;
- adore me;

- consider me good and acceptable;
- respect me; and
- love me.

Is there anyone who doesn't want these things? We love recognition. We love feeling seen by others in a positive light. Our Enemy knows this and wants to exploit it. In fact, he even appealed to these same desires when he tempted Jesus.

Prior to starting his earthly ministry, Jesus spent forty days in the desert being tempted by the devil. The devil was attempting to get Jesus to worship him because he knew that if he could get Jesus to sin, Jesus wouldn't be the pure, spotless Lamb that was required to cover our sins. Lucifer wanted the worship, and he wanted Jesus to fail.

> The devil led him up to a high place and showed him in an instant all the kingdoms of the world. And he said to him, "I will give you all their authority and splendor; it has been given to me, and I can give it to anyone I want to. If you worship me, it will all be yours."
>
> Jesus answered, "It is written: 'Worship the Lord your God and serve him only.'" (Luke 4:5–8)

Do you see how the devil tried to reproduce his pride and desire for worship in Jesus? He uses the same tactic on us because he wants worship-hungry people who will stop at nothing to get it. He wants us to not be okay without it because he is not okay without it. That's a definition of addiction right there. And today, there may be no better place for praise- and worship-hungry people to get their fix than on social media.

Enter Social Media

We're gonna go ahead and admit it now. We're grateful that social media exists! We met through social media, and we've had the privilege of cultivating our ministry, the Her True Worth community, through platforms like Instagram, Facebook, and Pinterest. Brittany and her husband, Ryan, actually met on Instagram too!

It's our firm belief that when it's used with wisdom and strong boundaries, social media is an awesome tool that can be used for the kingdom of God. For example, Her True Worth on Instagram and Facebook has been able to reach over five million people per month as of this writing (and growing). We believe that if you are breathing, you probably need some encouragement. So we set out to help encourage ladies all around the world with the gospel and bite-size daily devotions.

Social media is an incredible space for creatives to share their work, for writers to share their stories, for makers to share what they've made, and for people all over the world to connect, but we'd be naive to attempt discussing the wonders of social media without tackling the potential pitfalls these fun apps pose.

The Dark Side of Social Media

The devil is all up in the digital details.

If we're not aware of the tactics the Enemy uses on social media, we're unlikely to avoid the destructive and addictive behaviors these apps can result in. Not to mention the mindless scrolling these apps were intentionally designed to create—and the impact this has on our relationships, mental health, and our perception of reality itself.

The repetitive dopamine hits trigger the reward centers in our brains and ensure we'll keep coming back for more. We swipe in a downward motion similar to pulling the lever of a slot machine. Our gaze returns over and over again, looking for another hit.[6] We're hooked, and we don't even know it. *One more scroll*, we tell ourselves. *One more like. One more share.* Until no amount of social media consumption satisfies our hunger for affirmation.

We're going to keep it real simple: scrolling the feed was never intended to keep you fed. The internet cannot replace your pastor, and beautiful graphics with catchy phrases cannot replace your Bible. Although we can connect with people all over the world, we as a society have become increasingly isolated and lonely. We were never intended to bear the burden of having hundreds and sometimes thousands of strangers critiquing and consuming our lives for their entertainment. Not to mention the devastating damage these filtered images have on the development of impressionable youth.

Please don't misunderstand us: again, social media (or the internet) isn't inherently evil. What we do online matters, but it cannot become what matters most to us, or this little place on the internet will hold the power to devastate us.

Social media is an awesome tool! It has blessed us (Britt and Cass) with countless friendships and incredible opportunities, but it doesn't have the power to define us. When did people's lives become products of mass consumption? What message are we sending here? When did we become only as valuable as our latest post's performance? When did the ordinary moments of our lives become inferior to the highlight reels of someone else's carefully curated reality? It's easy to become dissatisfied, polarized, and desensitized when we live our lives through the blue haze of our screens.

Can we decide to do something that just might be revolutionary? Let's normalize spending less time curating content and more time cultivating contentment. Deal?

You might be asking, How do I cultivate contentment in a world that is constantly reminding me that I'm not enough and implores me to seek more of everything? Good question, friend. In his letter to the church at Philippi, the apostle Paul had some great things to say about contentment:

> I know what it is to be in need, and I know what it is to have plenty. I have learned the secret of being content in any and every situation, whether well fed or hungry, whether living in plenty or in want. I can do all this through him who gives me strength. (Philippians 4:12–13)

I (Cass) find this verse especially fascinating for two reasons. First of all, it was penned while Paul was in prison; and second, Paul spoke of the freedom found by being content in all circumstances. Hello, conviction! Although you and I might not be living our lives within the confines of a jail cell, is it possible we've been captured by the devices we carry and become prisoners of our own making? We're drawn to the dizzying blue glow of the screen like an insect is drawn into the pretty flicker of a bug zapper. Caution: guarding our hearts against discontentment is imperative. When we can find contentment in all circumstances, we're less likely to fall prey to the dark side of social media. When our hearts are truly satisfied in Christ, we're less likely to look to the affirmation of others to fill that void.

Practical Steps to Cultivate Contentment

- Create healthy boundaries with social media usage. Boundaries are a blessing, not a hindrance. We build boundaries around the things that matter to us. Guard your heart.
- Cultivate a heart of gratitude. As Bob and Larry from *VeggieTales* say, "A thankful heart is a happy heart."[7]
- Carefully curate your social media feeds with content through the lens of Philippians 4:8: "Finally, brothers and sisters, whatever is true, whatever is noble, whatever is right, whatever is pure, whatever is lovely, whatever is admirable—if anything is excellent or praiseworthy—think about such things."

The Effects of Social Media

We need to create boundaries around social media usage if we're going to avoid affirmation addiction. Excessive social media use can create a negative, self-perpetuating cycle. It also increases FOMO and feelings of inadequacy, dissatisfaction, and isolation. In turn, these feelings negatively affect our mood and worsen symptoms of depression, anxiety, and stress.

- "According to a 2017 Harris Poll, nearly two-thirds of Americans edit their photos before posting."[8] It's important to keep this in mind when viewing other people's posted images. Looking at edited photos can cause us to compare ourselves to an unobtainable standard that the original posters themselves couldn't achieve without Photoshop.
- A study of five thousand people published in the *American Journal of Epidemiology* found that higher social media use correlated with self-reported declines in mental and physical health and life satisfaction.[9] Pay attention to how you feel when using social media.
- The study found that features such as push notifications and scrolling create a feedback loop that keeps us glued to our devices.[10] We need to keep the intentionally addictive design of these apps in mind.
- A study by Yale psychologist Molly Crocket demonstrated that it's much easier to be outraged by other people's opinions when we can't see their faces and all we have to do is "like" a post that attacks them. An article from the

Atlantic tells us, "Crockett has argued, the normal forces that might stop us from joining an outrage mob—such as time to reflect and cool off, or feelings of empathy for a person being humiliated—are attenuated when we can't see the person's face, and when we are asked, many times a day, to take a side by publicly 'liking' the condemnation."[11] Although we have ability to connect with people all over the world, we've become dismissive of their human dignity and desensitized to cruelty online.

Two Reasons Affirmation from Others Will Never Satisfy

Again, the desire to be liked isn't inherently evil. We want to emphasize that God wired us to seek approval, but where we go wrong is when we seek it out in the wrong places. Because the fact remains: there is only one who can really approve of us, and *his* approval is enough.

God also built us to desire encouragement. The motives of our hearts determine the power that desire has—and the lengths we will go to meet that need. When we allow ourselves to become dependent on the acceptance and approval of others, we're in trouble. Why?

Reason 1: People Are Fickle

We totally get it. It feels *really* good to be well liked and have the approval of others. But remember this: people are fickle.

People change, and they change their minds. If your only avenue of affirmation is other people, you will always be living up to their changing feelings and opinions of you. One minute somebody can be following you on social media and admire the things you post, but then the next minute you post something they don't like and they hit the unfollow button. Or they cancel you.

I (Britt) remember when I first got an Instagram account back in 2011. It was a fresh new way to connect with people by using these little squares to showcase your life. I felt like a world-class Instagram photographer, showing everyone all the rad images on my phone using hashtags. Even though back then I'm not sure anyone really knew how to use a hashtag. #rememberwhenhashtagsweresentences?

A couple of years into using it, I found myself curious about an app that showed you who followed and unfollowed you on Instagram. After downloading it, I hurt my own dang feelings when I saw people unfollow me every day. But I couldn't stop checking! Once I was able to see, I couldn't stop looking. I became obsessed with checking it *all* the time and would actually get really hurt when people I thought were my friends chose to unfollow me for whatever reason. Why didn't they like me? What did I post that made them so unhappy to unfollow me? Also, why did I care so much?

Man, it was certainly a blow to my ego. I thought I was cool, and I thought people liked the stuff I shared. I thought they liked *me*. Yet being unfollowed made me feel rejected.

I quickly learned that placing my value in the opinions and

affirmation of others will never enable me to stand on solid ground. The truth is, you'll always be unfollowed, rejected, and disliked. Not everybody is going to love you, and therefore people loving you probably isn't the best choice to anchor your identity in. If you do, you'll always be tossed about, trying to keep up.

Reason 2: You Can't Keep Up

Take it from us, former people pleasers and recovering affirmation addicts: once you've obtained their approval, you'll do anything to keep it, and the pursuit of maintaining their approval is never-ending.

Take a look at trends. For example, can you honestly say that a pair of shoes you purchased fifteen years ago is still on trend today? Probably not, because trends are constantly changing. Except for on rare occasions when you can recycle a pair of nude heels that have been a staple item for a decade.

If you're into trends you know you've always gotta be keeping up with them. You also know that your wardrobe will never be fully on trend because by the time you think you've purchased everything to maintain the look you're going for, the trends will change again. Remember when Gen Z decided that skinny jeans were "cheugy" and high-waisted, straight-leg jeans were the new it thing? Oh, the outrage that ensued. According to Urban Dictionary, the term *cheugy* is defined as the "opposite of trendy."[12] But many of us millennials remember this hot style of denim as unflattering "mom jeans." It's comical. Often we see this cycle of trends repeating themselves every other decade or so. Out with the old, in with the new, and back with the old again.

Recently I (Britt) was looking at old family photos and giggling at the clothing choices in them. My mom's big, frizzy, outdated eighties hair in the nineties with high-rise, acid-wash jeans and her socks pulled up were considered *top notch* back in the day. Or my dad's curly mullet and hilariously thick mustache. When those pictures were taken, they probably fit right in with what was considered in fashion at the time. Yet, if they walked around looking like that today, they'd probably get double takes and laughs.

The Cost of Trying to Keep Up

I (Britt) have never personally taken an interest in watching the popular reality show *Keeping Up with the Kardashians*, but I do know some ladies who watch it. The show is known for being a ratings juggernaut and has become a cultural phenomenon. Our society often looks to the Kardashians and Jenners as the measuring stick and standard of beauty, fashion, and makeup. When I worked in the makeup industry, one of the most well-known facts in the industry was that the Kardashians were some of the biggest trendsetters. So much that Kylie Jenner launched a very successful lipstick brand that's valued at more than a billion dollars.

If you're familiar with the beauty industry at all, you know how quickly trends come and go—and sometimes repeat. It's exhausting to try to keep up! Must be nice to be a Kardashian so you're setting the gold standard rather than always trying to "keep up." (Still, we can imagine that setting the pace and constantly being under the public eye could be tiring in its own way. That's a lot of pressure.)

What if the desire to keep up is robbing us of the contentment in where we actually are? What if there's beauty in the unfrilly, the messy, and the imperfect? Guarding our hearts against discontentment helps us avoid the toll affirmation addiction takes on us, and it helps stop the cycle we find ourselves entangled in. Cultivating contentment is contagious. When we choose to be content in all circumstances, the freedom we have access to is evident in our lives—and it ushers others into the freedom for themselves.

The world needs your authentic self, not your best imitation of someone else. Who you are in Christ alone is so much more beautiful than your best-filtered photo.

Four Characteristics of Healthy Affirmation

We have to put affirmation in its rightful place in order to live a fruitful life. The affirmation we receive from others is an add-on to the confirmation we've already received from God through Jesus Christ's death, burial, and resurrection. This is an eternal issue, deeply rooted within the heart of every human being.

Let's break down what *healthy validation* looks like.

1. Healthy Affirmation Begins with God

No one but God has the authority to tell you who you are.

You aren't defined by the limitations or expectations of others. You're defined by who he is and what he did on the cross. No one can take that away from you. The more secure you are in Christ, the less likely you are to allow yourself to fall into the trap of popular opinion—because when everything changes, he remains the same. In truth, the only thing in life that remains the same is how inconsistent life is and how immovable our God is. We have the assurance of this promise from Scripture: "The grass withers and the flowers fall, but the word of our God endures forever" (Isaiah 40:8).

Seasons change, but God alone remains the same. Stop allowing the fickle opinions of people to dictate your life. Today is a good day to lay down the burden of carrying other people's opinions. Ain't nobody got time for that. Let Jesus handle it.

2. Healthy Affirmation Isn't Deterred by Rejection

The opposite of affirmation is rejection, and often the fear of rejection gets us chasing after affirmation in the first place.

Trust me; I (Cass) know what it feels like to be rejected. Sure, I might be coleading a ministry community that pours into millions of women all over the world today, but I've also been the girl who was eager to serve the women's ministry team at her local church only to never be invited to attend another meeting again. After multiple attempts at trying to connect with the women on the team via text, I got the message loud and clear: "There's no place for you here." I've experienced the sting that comes with the disapproval of my peers, and I've endured the pain of feeling like the calling on my life was being dismissed by those I held in high regard. I remember what it felt like to buy into the lie that my lack of experience and resources meant I was disqualified from being used by God. I've had my zeal for God misunderstood as selfish ambition and my God-given gift of creativity misinterpreted as pride seeking a pedestal.

Maybe you've walked through something similar.

Perhaps it wasn't within the walls of your church. Maybe it was a coworker, a teacher, a parent, or a spouse who rejected you, misunderstood your motives, and took it upon themselves to serve you a big ol' piece of humble pie. I can't pretend I know the reason you walked through the pain of rejection, but here's what I do know: rejection can redirect you, but it doesn't carry the authority to stop you.

Guess who was rejected more than any person alive? Jesus. Here is what the Bible says about how he was treated:

> He was despised and rejected by mankind,
>   a man of suffering, and familiar with pain.
> Like one from whom people hide their faces
>   he was despised, and we held him in low
>   esteem.
>
> Surely he took up our pain
>   and bore our suffering,
> yet we considered him punished by God,
>   stricken by him, and afflicted.

> But he was pierced for our transgressions,
>> he was crushed for our iniquities;
> the punishment that brought us peace was on him,
>> and by his wounds we are healed.
>
> (Isaiah 53:3–5)

The rejection Jesus faced did not affect who he was or what his assignment was. He knew that people were going to reject him, and yet he never wavered in his mission to secure our salvation. He hauled his cross past the hurling insults and accusations and continued on.

What if picking up our cross every day looks like that too? In the face of rejection, accusations, and shifting opinions, we remain firm and steadfast in what Christ did for us and who we are in him.

If we're living our lives to seek first the kingdom of God (Matthew 6:33), we cannot allow the threat of rejection to deter us. The sting of rejection inflicts pain like salt poured into a fresh wound, but it doesn't wield the power to destroy us. We can never outrun rejection. It's always going to be there. Jesus spoke the most life-giving words, and yet even he was still rejected. This proves yet again that we cannot earn our worthiness from the approval of people because their minds are always subject to change. In contrast, God gave us his approval while we were still sinners. Despite the fact that humanity rejected him, Jesus died for us (Romans 5:8).

Yes, rejection is always going to be there. In fact, Jesus said we should expect it:

> If the world hates you, keep in mind that it hated me first. If
> you belonged to the world, it would love you as its own. As it
> is, you do not belong to the world, but I have chosen you out
> of the world. That is why the world hates you. (John 15:18–19)

Because you'll never be able to escape rejection, you might as well seek affirmation from the only one who will never change his mind about you. Don't give up! Press on and persevere in the mighty name of Jesus!

I can tell you that my life is living proof that although people will dismiss you, God is faithful to direct you, and only God promotes you. Countless doors have shut in my face over the years, but every single time, God had an alternate route mapped out. If God has a path for you, trust him to redirect you.

The methods we use to acquire our worth determine the cost we commit to paying in our efforts to preserve that worth. Sounds exhausting, right? Friend, you deserve to stop working for your worth and start living secure in your identity in Christ.

3. Healthy Affirmation Practices Relational Equity

The loudest voices often get heard first, and sifting through the noise is difficult. That's why we need to use wisdom when deciding who has permission to speak into our lives. The weight of people pleasing is heavy, and it's a burden we were never intended to bear. Not every voice heard is a voice to heed. The wisdom of Scripture tells us to "guard your heart above all else, for it determines the course of your life" (Proverbs 4:23 NLT).

If we're not careful, we will drown in a sea of other people's opinions. God created us for connection and to live in community. So how do we decipher the difference between the voices to heed and the voices to leave?

First, we need to determine what my (Cass's) friend Toni Collier calls *relational equity*. Is this person a stranger, an acquaintance, a coworker, a friend, a confidant, a mentor, or a spouse? Determine the relationship you have with someone or the lack thereof; it's key to deciding the weight you'll place on their words in your life.

Here's what I'm *not* saying: "You're above reproach and therefore you shouldn't care about what other people have to say."

Here's what I *am* saying: "The context of the relationship defines the weight of their input in your life."

We all need wise counsel and accountability in our lives. As a matter of fact, the Bible expressly says that those without a multitude of wise counsel will fall (Proverbs 11:14). But receiving correction and direction from complete strangers is unwise. When you don't filter the voices that speak into your life, you're standing on dangerous ground. You're building your life upon the constantly shifting sands of popular opinion when God clearly tells us the wise build our lives upon his firm foundation (Matthew 7:24–27).

The truth is, we can care about what someone has to say about us without carrying their opinions with us everywhere we go.

I am the peacemaker in most of my friend groups. I have the weighty and often inconvenient ability to see multiple sides of every scenario. For this reason, I often find myself sitting on my couch and talking with my closest friends; they usually ask for my insight into difficult scenarios in their lives where they're trying to handle the unsolicited advice of others or navigate biblical boundaries. I always remind them of one simple thing I've learned to live by: if someone isn't willing to share my consequences, they have no place in the decisions I make with my life.

Simply said, "No consequences, no say."

This applies to much more than the unsolicited advice and opinions of strangers on the internet. This applies in all areas of our lives. Why? Because, as Toni wisely told me, "relational equity matters."

When you know how much someone has deposited into your life, that helps you determine the weight of their words in it. If you're going to speak into my life, you must first be willing to bear my burdens with me. This is both biblical (Galatians 6:2) and practical. As the saying goes, people don't care how much you know until they know how much you care.

I think this is something so many of us miss in this social-media-saturated world. Just because someone has access to you doesn't mean they have authority over you. It's important to evaluate if someone has earned the right to speak into your life.

If you don't guard your heart carefully, you will give people who aren't qualified the ability to make or break you with their opinions.

4. Healthy Affirmation Is Willing to Be Misunderstood

Sometimes the wisest thing you can do is give yourself permission to be misunderstood.

Does that mean I (Cass) don't care what people think? Of

course I care. If I'm being brutally honest here—which I am because I love you enough to tell you the truth—I probably care a little too much about what other people think of me. But I make the daily choice not to carry the weight of other people's opinions with me everywhere I go, and so should you. I do my best to take counsel from the apostle Paul, who wrote, "Am I now trying to win the approval of human beings, or of God? Or am I trying to please people? If I were still trying to please people, I would not be a servant of Christ" (Galatians 1:10).

Not everyone's opinion of you matters. We must accept the fact that some people will misunderstand us. A small number of voices will deeply matter in your life, and it's important to not allow all the noise of those who aren't invested in your life speak into it, drowning out those who do until you can no longer hear the difference. And what is the most important voice? The voice of God. Why do we continue to allow any voice to carry more value than God's?

So go ahead and give yourself permission. Look! We'll even give you a permission slip to do it.

I _____ have permission to listen to the voice of God above all others and filter my life through the Word of God instead of the opinions of others. I hereby grant myself permission to be misunderstood.

_____
Signature

_____
Date

It's time to break free from the endless cycle of affirmation addiction and find our approval in Christ alone. Let's ditch the filters and give up on trying to keep up. It's time to put some healthy boundaries on our relationship with social media and stop people pleasing. We're made for so much more than chasing after our worth in all the wrong places.

Reflect and Respond

1. Describe a time in your life when the desire for affirmation became unhealthy.
2. Have you believed a statement like this: "I'm more loved, accepted, and worthy if/when _____"? How did this affect you?
3. Do you use social media? If so, do you have healthy boundaries with your social media? If your answer is no, what do you think needs to change?
4. In what ways do you find the four characteristics of healthy affirmation challenging?

Four

Removing the Filter
Exposing the Real You

IT'S DIFFICULT TO STEP OUT from behind a filter—to feel confident in the real you—if your primary source of validation is in your appearance or image. That's why it's important to understand the depths of God's love for you through the power of his Word.

When it comes to embracing who we really are, our wider culture often encourages us to practice self-love or self-care. While there are merits to this, and it is biblical to practice self-care, there are also limits to what any self-initiated practice can do. To truly step out from behind the filters, we need to switch our focus from what we see in the mirror to what God sees when he looks at us.

Let's begin with defining self-care and self-love. It's important to understand the meaning of these terms.

What is *self-care*? "The practice of taking action to preserve or improve one's own health. The practice of taking an active role in protecting one's own well-being and happiness, in particular during periods of stress."[13]

What is *self-love*? "Regard for one's own well-being and happiness (chiefly considered as a desirable rather than narcissistic characteristic)."[14]

Superficial Solutions for Our Internal Struggle

Self-care will never truly satisfy, but when we look to Christ to sustain us, our cup will run over. When we drink from the well of self, we will never quench our thirst—because the truth is, self-love is a lesser love.

"You can't love others until you love yourself." "You can't give from an empty cup." We see messages like this all over the internet and social media along with aesthetically pleasing graphics, but is this sentiment true? What does the Bible say? The apostle Paul wrote that in the last days "people will be lovers of themselves . . . rather than lovers of God" (2 Timothy 3:2, 4).

Ouch.

I (Cass) don't like the sound of that. I'm stepping on my own toes here. Hello, conviction! Am I right?

True self-love is acknowledging our imperfections and identifying ourselves as a redeemed people. Yes, we are loved and accepted, but it's not because we are inherently good or worthy. We're imperfect and plagued by sin, but Christ is worthy. Only through Jesus can we accept the reality of redemption and discover our true worth. Through the redemptive work of the cross, we realize it's not all about us, and we begin to look upward.

Wait, hold up, Cass! Doesn't the Bible say we are "wonderfully made"? You're right! It does state that. Now let's take a look at the entirety of that scripture: "I praise you because I am fearfully and wonderfully made; your works are wonderful, I know that full well" (Psalm 139:14).

We praise God because he made us and his works are good. When we fix our eyes solely on loving what we see in the mirror, we fail to acknowledge the one who formed us. If we don't accept and acknowledge the love of God, we cannot hope to love ourselves or others well. There's no amount of self-care that can satisfy our souls' need for the tender love and care of God. These are the world's superficial solutions for our internal struggle. Our self-worth cannot be founded on our own worthiness! Self-love shifts and fades based on how we view ourselves, but the love of God is immovable and unchanging. This is why our understanding of self-love needs to change. This is why our self-worth cannot be founded on our own worthiness. Self-love isn't a sustainable love. The love of self is unstable, but the love of God endures forever.

We were made in *God's image* (Genesis 1:26–27). Let that sink in. Isn't that incredible? No wonder the Enemy makes it so dang hard to love the skin we're in. To love ourselves rightly requires first loving the one whose image we were made to reflect. Not the person staring back at us in the mirror.

The Lord declares we are all wonderfully made. I finally decided to believe him. Not because I suddenly discovered self-love but rather because I found the love of the Creator, and I trust that he doesn't make mistakes. I believe that the fight to love the skin I'm in isn't just against my thoughts but also against the Enemy of my soul. The Enemy wants us to believe that God's love is superficial and conditional like the love the world offers us, but, the truth is, the love of God isn't skin deep. It's soul deep.

The battle is continuous, but the love of God already conquered the gates of hell to win my heart. It's an intentional, daily choice to believe God's thoughts over my own. I am who he says I am. I'm forgiven. I'm not defined by my past, my cellulite, or my flaws. His love defeated my guilt and shame. His love rescued me from myself. He did it for me, and I know he'll do it for you, too, if you'll let him. Our identity, validation, and worth must be found in Christ alone. Nothing else can truly fill your cup. And when he fills your cup, it will run over (Psalm 23:5).

I've fallen into the thought process of "I'll be happy when I'm a size _____." This is shallow and untrue. We cannot find our self-worth or happiness in our size. There is no such thing as a "size happy." Large or small, Jesus loves us all. Friend, please stop looking for your validation in the mirror or on a scale. Your identity cannot be found there no matter how long you stare. Your worth cannot be found on the tag inside your jeans or leggings. Your beauty cannot be measured. Your appearance does not define you. Your identity is found in something that no one but God can truly see.

Check out what God said when the prophet Samuel saw

David's impressive elder brother and thought Eliab must be the man God had chosen to be king:

> The LORD said to Samuel, "Do not consider his appearance or his height, for I have rejected him. The LORD does not look at the things people look at. People look at the outward appearance, but the LORD looks at the heart." (1 Samuel 16:7)

God looks at the heart. Your weight will fluctuate, your body will change, but his love for you remains the same. Your body is a vessel. It's a tool. It does not determine your value. Only Christ can do that. Your body is not an object for others to look at for pleasure. Your identity is safely hidden in God's care. The apostle Paul said it this way: "You died to this life, and your real life is hidden with Christ in God" (Colossians 3:3 NLT). No amount of Photoshop can change who we are in Christ. It's time to remove the filters we hide behind and allow God to reveal our identity in him.

Turn the Light On

I (Cass) want to share a little story about something that happened to me during lockdown. But first, I need to admit that it's about a very simple inconvenience. While this was a challenging period for all of us to some degree, we want to acknowledge that it was also traumatic for some—especially those who lost loved ones, suffered financial insecurity, endured long-term school closures, or worked on the frontlines in health care and essential services. If this is the case for you, know that we understand this, that we see you. And if you're one of the many thousands who had trouble finding plumbers, electricians, and other services during the lockdown, we see you too. Except we couldn't see you during the lockdown. Because our lights were out.

My husband and I went without an overhead light in our master bathroom for what seemed like an eternity. There was some problem with the wiring that only an electrician could fix. It had only been a couple of weeks, but it felt like we were fumbling around in the dark for much longer. We put in a work order just at the exact moment that the COVID-19 pandemic hit our little corner of Oklahoma. Due to the lockdown, we were placed on a waiting list for an electrician to access our situation. In the meantime, I had been functioning for so long without light while getting ready for the day that I started to begin missing things in the mirror that I'd otherwise have noticed. We weren't leaving the house often during this time, but when I did manage to leave and caught a glimpse of myself in the rearview mirror of my car, it was hilarious. I was a hot mess, and it was laughable. Our dark and dingy master bathroom had become our normal because I had become accustomed to the lack of light. As a result, I wasn't seeing myself clearly, and I was leaving the house looking wildly disheveled.

The Word of God is our light. We need it to navigate life. Just like someone looking at a dirty mirror in a dimly lit room, we cannot see ourselves or others clearly without light. Clear sight is only possible when we immerse ourselves in God's Word and intentionally follow through on what it says. When we read our Bibles daily, we can turn the light on in our lives and see things clearly. Through the power of his Word, our hearts are cleansed and purified. Through him, the blind can see (Isaiah 29:18). Be careful not to become comfortable living without the light the Bible sheds in your life. You will miss important details.

The Enemy will always poke and prod at the things that ache the most. He will use our insecurities to inflict further pain if left unchecked. This is why it's so important to take our thoughts captive and make them obedient to Christ (2 Corinthians 10:5).

Have you ever experienced an intrusive thought? An intrusive thought is something that randomly pops into your mind without warning and is often disheartening or distressing. When we experience these sorts of mental and spiritual attacks, it's important that we combat these dark thoughts with the clarity the Bible offers. The Enemy cannot pit you against the Word of God without your permission. The Word of God is our ultimate weapon against the Enemy's schemes.

The Word of God is a lamp to our feet, guiding us through the darkness that attempts to overcome us (Psalm 119:105). You must refuse to despise what God has called good. We cannot come into agreement with our Enemy; we must stand firm in the truth of who we are and whose we are. We must love what God loves and hate what he hates.

Beloved, it's our sincere prayer that by the time you finish reading this book, you're going to walk triumphant and confident in who God is and who you are in him. Nothing else matters.

I've learned many of life's lessons the hard way, and I'm here to tell you: I know God is faithful because I've been left with nothing but faith to hold on to. I know God provides because I've seen him provide a way where we could see no other way. I know he will never leave or forsake me because I know the sting of rejection and abandonment. I know from experience that he is a Father to the fatherless. I know he redeems and restores because my life has been transformed. I know the depth of God's love is more than skin deep because I've experienced it for myself. I know religion can't save but a relationship with Christ is the only way. Through him, we're all empowered to live unfiltered and radically free.

I want you to know this for yourself. Turn on the light in your life and turn to God's Word. He will tell you how he feels about you. He will give you wisdom. He will send his Spirit to speak into your heart. You won't have to squint in the dark anymore. God himself will provide a lamp for your feet and a light for your path.

Beauty Redefined

I (Cass) was a hair and makeup artist for more than ten years before God called me to put down my shears in exchange for a pen. When I was behind the chair, I became more than just a hairstylist. I was a trusted confidant—a therapist and a friend! I was a highly sought-after colorist, specializing in balayage and lived-in color when ombre was all the rage. My clients would book weeks and months in advance to secure their coveted hairapy appointment. We'd laugh and cry together as I rinsed out their violet toner. I'd smile and nod as I pretended to hear them while my Paul Mitchell blow dryer's volume whirred at full blast!

During the decade I did hair and makeup, I had the privilege of witnessing the transformative power of self-confidence. Countless women entered my salon, heads hung low, feeling insecure and defeated. My favorite part of my job was the grand reveal. As a young apprentice, I was trained to intentionally dry and style my clients with their backs facing the mirror; but oh, when that chair turned. It was like a light switch had been turned on, and these women were seeing themselves for the very first time. They were giddy and full of excitement to see themselves new and improved. Although this gave them a huge emotional rush, this type of beauty is fleeting. The woman who left the salon with fresh hair was still the very same woman who'd driven herself there. The only difference was how she saw herself. Glamour fades, trends change, and beauty standards give us whiplash; but a woman who fears the Lord is truly beautiful (Proverbs 31:30).

The transformation my clients experienced was a parlor trick. It was a temporary confidence boost that would ultimately leave them looking for another fix in four to six weeks. We're tackling an internal issue with external solutions, leading to eternal repercussions. Putting on makeup, applying skin-care products, and undergoing outward modifications are no different. We're attempting to cover up our imperfections that are ultimately the outward expression of the fallen world we live in. Over time our bodies deteriorate and decay. Skin begins to lack its youthful luster. It's called *concealer* for a reason. Aesthetics aren't inherently evil, but it's all about the motives of our hearts.

Roses, Receipts, and Redemption

One of the things that often keeps us from being our true selves is shame about our past. I (Cass) understand that because I've had to overcome that kind of shame myself.

I remember sitting in a crowded auditorium, shoulder to shoulder with my peers, as a man and his wife shared what would be my first experience with purity culture. I was fresh out of high school and cautiously dipping my toes into this Christianity thing. As someone who wasn't raised in a believing household, I was still dealing with the aftershock of living deep within the Bible Belt, where Scripture saturated every aspect of life. I shifted uncomfortably in my chair as this man shared a message on the beauty of purity, and I listened as he compared a woman's body to her righteousness. I was too young and naive to question this dude's theology, so I basically soaked it all in. I'll never forget the moment his wife stepped onstage and handed him a red rose.

He held the rose up and said, "This is a beautiful red rose. It's valuable and untouched." He then handed it to a boy sitting in the front row and asked him to smell it, touch its petals, and pass it to the person next to him and so on and so forth. This behavior continued during the entirety of his sermon until everyone in the room had experienced the beauty of the rose. When his message concluded he signaled his wife to walk back up to the stage with what was once a fresh and unblemished rose. He held it up in front of the room of at least two hundred college-aged kids and proclaimed, "Do you see this? What was once beautiful and without blemish has now been passed around and is now wilted. This is what happens when you lose your purity. This is what happens when you give yourself away. You get passed around, and no one wants to buy a wilted rose."

His statement startled me. I identified with this withered and undesirable rose, and I couldn't help but wonder: Was that truly how God viewed me? This question rippled into my life in many ways in the years that followed. My virginity was still technically intact at that point in my life, but my purity had been tarnished and my innocence stolen from me without my consent many years prior. If you can relate to my experience, I want to tell you, God redeems the wilted roses and restores their beauty despite the damage done. God doesn't cast shame on those of us who have endured trauma at the hands of others. Nor does he keep a record of our own wrongs. When we accept Jesus as our Lord and Savior, his sacrifice wipes the slate clean and makes us white as snow (Isaiah 1:18).

I'd like to believe that this speaker had every good intention for this ridiculous demonstration, but I can't help but wonder, did the damage done outweigh any potentially positive results? In many ways the message that women's bodies, the way we dress, and purity are equal to our value and worth is still being perpetuated today. I'm a grown woman, and I'm still dismantling this lie for myself and for the sake of my children. If you've been led to believe this damaging narrative, I want to encourage you: nothing can be further from the truth. In the wise words of my friend Jess Connolly, "Shame off you."[15] Jesus came to save you, not to cast shame upon you.

There's a beautiful story in the Bible that demonstrates how God loves us even in the midst of our shame. Let's talk about the story of Hosea and Gomer. But I want to take a moment here to address the deeply troubling notion that a woman could be bought, and that a man could presume to know what price was right to pay for her. Although Gomer voluntarily solicited her body, her worth and value as *imago Dei* (image of God) was inherent and was never for sale.

Gomer was Hosea's wife. She left him over and over again to willingly return to her old life of prostitution. She gave herself to the highest bidder, selling herself cheaply, and yet Hosea purchased her at full price by paying off the man she was with. He knew what she had done and with whom, and yet he purchased Gomer as if she were untarnished because to him she was worth a costly, sacrificial love. This story mirrors the story of the Israelites and God, but I can't help but wonder if it strikes similarities within our own wandering hearts.

Hosea offered Gomer the type of love that knows your sin but calls you by name. The type of love that transcends your mistakes and redeems your shame. Sweet friend, that same love is accessible to you today. You will never know how treasured you truly are until you understand the depth of God's love for you.

God sees you for who you truly are. (Luke 16:15)

He knows you, and yet he still loves you. (Romans 5:8;
   1 Corinthians 8:3)

You're no longer a slave to sin. (Romans 6:6)

You are debt-free and loved. (1 John 1:9)

The love of God ruins the appeal of any lesser love. His love is the type of love that destroys counterfeits and redeems what we thought was supposed to be.

Jesus has the receipts, and guess what? He tossed them out! He knows what he purchased on Calvary, and he has no buyer's remorse. He knows where you've been, and he's seen what you've done. He doesn't require perfection for redemption, only your heart.

You are loved regardless of your past and can therefore have confidence in who you are in Christ today. Your past doesn't define you. You don't have to hide in shame. He died for the real you. Despite any wounds or insecurities you might have, he loves you fully. You are his rose and the apple of his eye. And though he redeems and accepts you, he doesn't just leave you where you are. He continues to free you from the wounds of the past.

Insecurity Is a Learned Behavior

It's been said that the wound passes through the womb. According to an article in *Psychology Today*, "All the eggs a woman will carry form in her ovaries while she is a *fetus* in *her mother's womb*.

In other words, when your mother was in your grandmother's womb, she carried, at that time, the egg that eventually became *you*. This means that a part of you, your mother, and your grandmother all shared the same biological environment. In a sense, you were exposed to the emotions and experiences of your grandmother even before you were conceived."[16]

There's a reason that families with a known history of unresolved trauma, abuse, addiction, anxiety, and depression are statistically more likely to be susceptible to the same struggles. This is known as transgenerational trauma. The suffering and trauma endured by one individual is often inherited by future generations until someone chooses to break the cycle. The same concept can be applied to generational sin. We are likely to repeat what we don't repair. If generational sin and trauma is passed down through decades of pain, perhaps healing can be inherited. As a mother of three, I (Cass) firmly believe that a mother who exudes confidence in Christ will influence her children to do the same. Children are better imitators than they are listeners.

Have you met a toddler? They can't stand to be told how to live their lives. Full transparency: I can totally relate. Despite my best efforts to get my children presentable in the mornings, my three-year-old insists on walking around the house in mismatched socks with cereal on his pj's, and he behaves as if he's invincible. We aren't born inherently insecure, my friend. Insecurity is a learned behavior, passed down from generation to generation. I'm here to tell you that this cycle can be broken in the mighty name of Jesus.

Imagine the type of world we'd live in if we all decided

to shed the things we hide behind, living secure in our worth and confident in our God-given identity. How would your life change if this truth became your reality? Imagine it with me for a moment. Leaving a group chat and not worrying about what people might be saying about you. Walking by a reflective surface without avoiding the sight of your own reflection. Reading the words of an internet troll without being wounded by their insults. When we place our worth in Christ, this type of unwavering confidence is possible.

To the girl who is afraid to shed the filters she hides behind, you can't outrun insecurity, but you can run into the arms of our Father and become totally secure in him. People might try to minimize you and make you feel inadequate, but they'll never be able to shrink the God of all capacity within you. Understanding the depth of God's love for us in a superficial world requires us to be fully immersed in his Word. Our confidence has to come from God himself.

We're able to step out from behind the filters we hide behind in confidence because we know that even when we are fully exposed, we are fully known and loved by God.

Exposing the Real You

As we previously discussed, self-care is both biblical and practical. But there are limits to what any self-initiated practice can do. If we want to truly care for ourselves, we must first prioritize caring for our souls. We have to turn our gaze upward and focus on how God sees us. Our primary source of validation and care cannot be placed on the desire to show up for ourselves, but rather it must be firmly founded on how Christ showed us his love for us through the cross.

We can't fully care for ourselves because we can't fully see ourselves in a dim and dingy mirror. Searching God's Word for his wisdom is what's really going to get us what we are looking for in self-love and self-care. Acknowledging our imperfections and bringing them to Jesus is soul-care.

A gentle reminder: glamour fades, beauty trends change and give us whiplash, but a woman who fears the Lord is truly beautiful (Proverbs 31:30).

You're not a wilted rose. God paid a steep price to have you as his own. He wants more than a skin-deep transformation for you. He wants to redeem and heal your soul. Through him, you're empowered to live your life totally exposed, unfiltered, and radically free. Perhaps the ultimate self-care is allowing God to care for you by healing your past wounds and taking away your insecurities, replacing them with his love.

Reflect and Respond

1. Do you practice self-care? If so, how? Is the concept of soul-care a practice you're willing to implement into your daily life? If so, in what ways will you care for your soul moving forward?

2. Do you define yourself by the standards of the world instead of the Word? If so, you're not alone! When we find ourselves dealing with doubt and uncertainty, we need to bring it to God. Try it! Take a moment and tell him what you're struggling with.

3. Have you allowed the shame of your past to define you? If so, how has this affected your life?

4. What is your earliest memory of battling insecurity? Do you feel like insecurity is an issue you currently struggle with? If so, how will you combat insecurity moving forward?

Five

Prodigal Daughter
Wounded and Wandering

JESUS' PARABLE OF THE PRODIGAL son is one of the most popular parables in the Bible (Luke 15:11–32). It is the story of a wealthy father with two sons. When the younger son asked his father to give him his inheritance early, even before his father's death, the father agreed. The younger son ran off to a distant land and immediately squandered all his money with wild, foolish living. Not very long thereafter, the son eventually hit rock bottom. His distraction, pride, and self-preservation got the better of him. Right around the time his money ran out, a famine broke out in the country, and he was starving. Driven by hunger and desperation, the son was forced to find work with a local farmer who sent him out to the fields to feed the pigs.

He reached such a low point that he was willing to steal and eat the pig's food out of the pig's trough. Yes, you heard that right—he stole and ate the scraps for pigs. He was alone, starving, and emptied. Can you imagine the shame he felt? The embarrassment? Here you have a young man who once had all he ever needed, and he wandered away from the life he knew and wasted it all.

We've probably all had our pig-trough moments—low points when we realize how far we've wandered from God. But, as we'll see, the pig trough was not the end of the story for the prodigal son, and it's not the end for us either.

Wandering Away from God

I (Britt) remember the first time I realized I had wandered away from God in my heart. Like the prodigal son, I had everything I could have ever needed because I had Jesus. I was saved and set free, but somehow along my journey I wandered right back into sin and deception.

I was partying a lot, harming my body, and very often tearing others down to make myself feel better. I can't really explain how I let myself get there because, the truth is, I don't think there's ever one single defining moment when we turn away from God and begin to wander. I think each wrong step away from God is another temptation from the Enemy that makes the distance between us and God a lot bigger.

My attention was not on God anymore. My focus became diverted to the flashiness and lust of the world. Reading my

Bible and spending time with the Lord every day wasn't my priority anymore. Gravitating toward worldly passions will always cost you in your relationship with Christ. We can't have one foot in the kingdom and one in the world. But I was sitting on the fence with one foot on each side.

The apostle John wrote:

> Do not love the world or anything in the world. If anyone loves the world, love for the Father is not in them. For everything in the world—the lust of the flesh, the lust of the eyes, and the pride of life—comes not from the Father but from the world.
> (1 John 2:15–16)

Read that again. "Do not love the world." I have to admit that I did love parts of the world. Straddling the fence only amplifies temptations, pulling us into a world we aren't meant to live in.

My faith in Christ was not rooted and grounded because I wasn't diving into Scripture and prioritizing Jesus. I didn't receive his Word upon fertile soil, and I hadn't done what was necessary to build on a good foundation (Matthew 13:1–8; 7:24–27). Because of this, the Enemy had a field day with me.

I squandered the grace that was so freely bestowed upon me. I stopped taking this "Jesus thing" so seriously. My eyes were clouded, and my ears only heard the screaming temptations of my flesh. I listened to lies:

- *Gossip about this person because you don't want people to like her more than they like you.*

- *Lie or exaggerate in ways that benefit you.*
- *Drink alcohol to drown out your feelings.*
- *Do whatever is necessary to be the most beautiful woman in the room because being highly desirable equals worthiness.*

Because my eyes were off Jesus, the world and opinions of others became the source of my satisfaction. Gratifying the desires of my flesh became as easy as breathing. My worth was all tangled up in it. I really had no idea who I was and how much I had lost sight of myself. In fact, I didn't even have the revelation that what I was doing was wrong and that I was living in sin. Backsliding will do that to you.

If you're not familiar with the term *backsliding*, it's defined as "to lapse morally or in the practice of religion."[17] It is tragically common in the body of Christ. We fall away and slide back into our old ways, disregarding the truth we once lived in. But we are called to leave all that behind.

The apostle Paul wrote:

You were taught, with regard to your former way of life, to put off your old self, which is being corrupted by its deceitful desires; to be made new in the attitude of your minds; and to put on the new self, created to be like God in true righteousness and holiness. (Ephesians 4:22–24)

There are two very important things to consider in this verse. The first is that *we are called to not only put off our old self but to put on the new self.* That means a new identity, with changed thinking. It means being led by God's Spirit and motivated by his love in every action. The verses above are some of my favorite verses concerning identity. The old self has to do with our flesh because our physical bodies have carnal instincts. Our old selves have lusts and desires that we will battle until the day our Lord comes back. That's why it's so important to take every thought captive and make it obedient to Christ (2 Corinthians 10:5).

The second thing to note from the passage is that the new self is something we get when we are born again, but *we have to put it on daily.* I wish this was a one-time event, but it is anything but. Just as we get dressed every day, we must put on our new selves each day like fresh, clean clothing. The new self is an identity wrapped in righteousness and holiness, renewed in knowledge after the image of our Savior. Paul instructed us to "walk by the Spirit, and you will not gratify the desires of the flesh. For the desires of the flesh are against the Spirit, and the desires of the Spirit are against the flesh, for these are opposed to each other, to keep you from doing the things you want to do" (Galatians 5:16–17 ESV).

He also went on to say:

> But the fruit of the Spirit is love, joy, peace, forbearance, kindness, goodness, faithfulness, gentleness and self-control. Against such things there is no law. Those who belong to Christ Jesus have crucified the flesh with its passions and desires. Since we live by the Spirit, let us keep in step with the Spirit. (Galatians 5:22–25)

As I backslid, I fell more and more out of step with the Spirit. In fact, I stepped right into addiction, lust, self-obsession, gossip, pride, and partying. Of course, in my heart, I still had love for Jesus. I knew that he was my Savior, but I took my life into my own hands and turned my eyes from the very source of my life. I forgot my need for a Savior.

I didn't see that I needed saving. I was deceived and unable to see things clearly because of the scales on my eyes. Like Paul in Acts 9:18, my spiritual vision was impaired. I wasn't able to grapple with the weight of my sin because my focus was on one thing: self. When I opened my Bible, I would be burned by the verses that direct us not to live according to the flesh but to die to ourselves (Romans 8:13). My distraction, pride, and self-preservation unquestionably got the better of me.

As in the story of the prodigal son, I, too, went through famine. Maybe not in the sense of being without food, but I was depleted body and soul. I found myself drawn to anything that gave me a sense of gravity or validity, compromising the truth of who I was in Christ. Like the prodigal son being willing to eat out of the pig's trough, I was willing to saturate myself in anything that made me feel "fed" and satisfied in my worth. I was selling myself cheap, though I knew I was bought at the highest price (1 Corinthians 6:19–20).

It's so dangerous to get in such a state of depletion that we'll desperately grab at anything the Enemy dangles in front of us because we have the notion that it will somehow fulfill us. We see this all over our world. Everyone seeks to be admired because the opinions of others are used as a measuring stick of worthiness.

But the truth is, when we look to anything other than Jesus to fill our cups, our cups will always run dry. We'll never be fully satisfied until we look to him.

Feeling empty and aware of the gaping hole inside of me, I realized something was very wrong. I questioned my own self-worth, my very existence. I didn't know who I was. I felt so deep in despair and lost, wandering in what seemed like the dark woods all alone without a glimmer of light or hope around me. I was suicidal and living in deep shame. There were many nights when I'd cry on my bathroom floor because I felt so worthless and alone. Nobody knew what was going on inside me, and I concealed it well. I would look into the mirror and not even recognize the person who was staring back at me. I hated my body, I hated myself, and I hated the person I had become. I had wandered so far away from Jesus and back into my former ways. I didn't want to confront the obvious truth that I had parted with him in my heart. I had turned my face away from him, which left me feeling hollow.

I had allowed myself to backslide into "worldly" thought patterns:

I can do this on my own.
I can guide myself.
I know what's best for me.

Sound familiar?

It's that place of depending on our own strength, our own understanding, which the Bible cautions us against.

> Trust in the LORD with all your heart,
>> and do not lean on your own understanding.
> In all your ways acknowledge him,
>> and he will make straight your paths.
> Be not wise in your own eyes;
>> fear the LORD, and turn away from evil.
> It will be healing to your flesh
>> and refreshment for your bones.
> (Proverbs 3:5–8 ESV)

Depending on our own strength leads to the search to feed and gratify our souls with anything that is thrown to us. Money, diets, sex, relationships, addiction, success—none of it will suffice in comparison to Christ in us, the hope of glory (Colossians 1:27).

Realizing the insecure place I found myself in, I began to wonder: *Why does God feel so far away?* The truth was, I was the one who had stepped away and was far from him. Don't we all ask ourselves that from time to time? *Why does God seem distant? Why isn't God answering me?*

Well, the truth is this: if God feels distant, he isn't the one who moved.

God is always giving 110 percent, and his hands are always extended to us. Maybe we can't hear him answering because we aren't taking the time and patience to listen. When we tend to the noise and static all around us, we become desensitized to the sound of his voice. We know that the Lord is close to the brokenhearted (Psalm 34:18) and that if we draw close to God, he draws close to us (James 4:8). Again, God is always reaching out, but are we?

If the Enemy cannot destroy you, he will try to keep you distracted with the noisiness of the world. God has a still, small voice (1 Kings 19:12). We need to be better about turning down the noise and distraction so we can position ourselves to hear what he is speaking to us.

Living in the deception of the world highlighted this one simple, yet freeing truth for me: *Jesus is truly the only one that can satisfy my aching, human heart. Nothing else can.* I could have searched to the ends of the earth trying to find myself, but all I needed was the one who gave himself for me: Jesus. He was speaking to me, calling me by name. He was calling me up and into his arms. However, I couldn't hear him because my mind was not on him but on myself. We are prodigal daughters anytime we search for unconditional love and acceptance in anything other than the Lord Jesus Christ.

The Return

When the prodigal son hit rock bottom, he made the decision to go back to his father and reconcile, asking forgiveness for all he had done. We might expect that the father would have been judgmental and maybe even rejected the son, but look how Jesus described the father's response: "While he was still a long way off, his father saw him and was filled with compassion for him;

he ran to his son, threw his arms around him and kissed him" (Luke 15:20).

Wow! Can you imagine the father's joy at seeing his lost son had returned? But how was the lost son's father able to see him from so far away? *Because he was looking for him.* Imagine his arms wide open, tears of joy in his eyes. As a parent, I (Britt) know how I would feel in that situation. I'd be heartbroken. I'd be searching every day for my child. What a beautiful illustration of the heart of our heavenly Father! Even when we were lost, *he never lost sight of us.* Because that is what a loving, compassionate Father does.

The prodigal son's father wasn't judgmental toward him upon his return. He didn't take an incriminating tone; he was just ecstatic, filled with love and compassion. His lost son had finally come home. His lost son was now found. His heart was thankful to God.

Beloved, God is not an "I can't believe you've done this" kind of God. Instead, he's the kind of God who says:

Come here.
Welcome home.
I'll keep you safe.
I'll keep you warm.
Let me hold you.
Let me heal you.
Let me celebrate you.
Let me vindicate you.
Let me transform you.

I love you.
I have so much for you.
I am not mad at you.
Trust me.
Look to me.
I will never leave you.
I will never give up on you.
My grace will never waver.
Stay with me.

When the father saw his son, he *ran*—he didn't walk—and embraced him and kissed him. The father had so much compassion in his heart that he never thought twice about why his son had gone away in the first place. After their warm welcome-home embrace, the son cried out and said, "Father, I have sinned against heaven and against you. I am no longer worthy to be called your son" (Luke 15:21).

The father's response to his son's apology wasn't to list all the things his son had done to wrong him, as if he had been keeping a record. He didn't rehash or revisit how his son had messed up.

But the father said to his servants, "Bring quickly the best robe, and put it on him, and put a ring on his hand, and shoes on his feet. And bring the fattened calf and kill it, and let us eat and celebrate. For this my son was dead, and is alive again; he was lost, and is found." And they began to celebrate. (Luke 15:22–24 esv)

The father threw a massive party for his found son. Again, a beautiful parallel to our heavenly Father's love toward us. Scripture says there is rejoicing in the presence of the angels of God over one sinner who repents (Luke 15:10). Now that we see the great depth of God's love and forgiveness, we get to extend it to others.

Living Forgiven and Forgiving Others

Contrary to what we have been taught to believe about religion, our heavenly Father has a heart to save and forgive rather than to punish or scold. When he forgives, he also forgets the wrong we've done (Hebrews 10:17). As we repent of our ways and turn from our sin, he covers over our sin. He doesn't lose sight of who he created us to be, even on the darkest days.

Our fallible minds can't even fathom a love that doesn't record each wrong done to it. Imagine a love that treats others according to their worth in Christ instead of the mistakes they've made. We are called to live in that same kind of love. We are called to model this same love and forgiveness to those who do us wrong. We are called to be living proof of God's love. The apostle Paul wrote, "Bear with each other and forgive one another if any of you has a grievance against someone. Forgive as the Lord forgave you" (Colossians 3:13).

Listen—we live in such a broken, offended, and hurting world. We create walls and unloving boundaries with each other, especially after someone has messed up or has committed a heinous act toward us. We build walls to protect ourselves from future pain. It makes sense to respond this way because we don't want to feel pain. But unforgiveness is poison. It hurts the one who drinks it.

Love keeps no record of the wrong done to it (1 Corinthians 13:5). Imagine if we sinned against God, then came back to him with a convicted heart and he had a wall up with us. Or because we had done so much wrong, he created a boundary to protect himself from us. That sounds strange, right? Pretty hard to imagine since that is so outside of his character. Should it not sound just as strange as a behavior coming from us, since we are called to imitate him (Ephesians 5:1)? No, we are not God, but we are certainly called to love like him. In fact, it's a commandment to love your neighbor as yourself (Matthew 22:39).

God's love is the love that embraces, hopes, perseveres, and has compassion in every circumstance. Love lays its life down for others. We can't withhold forgiveness when we have received so much that its overflowing. That would be super hypocritical. When I (Britt) think about all the sin I have committed in my lifetime and all the forgiveness I have received, it becomes easier to extend forgiveness to others. Whenever I struggle to forgive someone, I do this: Imagine holding five thousand small boxes stacked in your arms. You would be dropping them everywhere, trying to keep balance, and it would look like a silly mess. Boxes everywhere. That's all the forgiveness we have received and then some. Reach down, grab one, and give it to someone who needs it. Yes, they don't deserve it, but then again neither did we. That's grace.

Forgiveness does not mean you're enabling bad behavior

or that you now trust that person. Please hear me on that—especially in cases of physical and emotional abuse. Forgiveness given through you doesn't always mean access to you. But forgiveness does have power to free you from the offense committed against you. Learning how to forgive the way our Father forgives means offense doesn't have to dictate who you are at the end of the day because your identity is found in him—not in how others treat or mistreat you.

Stay with God

Imagine the prodigal son's disposition upon his return. He was most likely preparing himself for some harsh discipline from his father. After all, his share of the inheritance was now officially squandered. He knew he'd messed up and probably prepared his heart for the worst kind of punishment. I (Bitt) know I would have. The son confessed to what he had done, ready for whatever retribution came next. But there was not one word of condemnation from his father. Instead, the father dressed him in fine clothing and placed a ring on his finger. Surely the prodigal son felt unworthy, but all the father wanted him to do was to return home to his family where he belonged. Jesus didn't say this in the parable, but I would like to think that the father had forgiveness in his heart toward his son the moment he left home.

The son's heart posture wasn't to return as a son but as a worker and a servant. While he was still on his far-away journey, he reasoned, *My father's workers get treated better than this. I will return as a worker in humility, realizing my low position. I'm not going back to reclaim a safe and comfy spot as a son, but I realize I have nothing, and I need to go home* (Luke 15:19).

The son had a humble and repentant heart. He knew he had made a grave mistake, and he didn't have a heart of entitlement. God's mercy is magnified even more when we return to him with a heart of repentance, humility, and realizing our need for him. When we hit bottom and realize our desperate need for God, the only place we want to be is home. We've all been in that wandering place. That place we swore to ourselves we'd never fall back into once we dedicated our lives to Christ. Sadly, some of us stay in that place, thinking there's no possible way that God could take us back after what we've done. We are hesitant to be exposed to the light—his light—because of all the things we allowed to pile up in the darkness.

Surrendering every broken part of ourselves feels like a mountain of a task that is just too unbearable to take on, so we resist and isolate from him. But "if we confess our sins, he is faithful and just to forgive us our sins and to cleanse us from all unrighteousness" (1 John 1:9 ESV).

If this is you today, give him your burdens (Psalm 55:22). Come back to God, and stay with him. Like the loving father in the story of the prodigal son, our heavenly Father is also watching and waiting for all who have turned away to come back home to him. He is always keeping a close eye on his people, whether it's for a child returning home or for a heart not yet surrendered.

Maybe that's you today. Maybe you've wandered off and you're looking around and asking yourself:

How did I get here?
Why do I feel so empty?
Why does God feel so far away?

I want to encourage you with this: He has not left or abandoned you. It doesn't matter what you've done or where you've been or how far you've wandered away. His door is open to you.

I vividly remember when I turned my eyes back on God after wandering away. I was afraid that he was going to reject me and not want me anymore. What a lie that the Enemy tells us to keep us from running back to God! I knew I had squandered his grace, just like the prodigal son squandered his inheritance. I felt so much guilt and shame, I couldn't imagine God taking me back and still loving me. After all I had done? No way. But he did. *He took me back.* He kissed me with his grace. His arms embraced me, and it was as though distance between us had never existed.

I realized that life without Christ will always leave me wounded and wandering down paths I was never meant to travel down. See, his goodness is designed to lead us into changed and repentant hearts. Understanding God's love and goodness is key to understanding who we are in him so we can grow in our relationship with him.

But remember, friend, *faith* and *trust* are required. No turning back. No U-turn.

You won't always feel valuable to God. The Enemy blatantly attacks our feelings and tries to convince us that what we "feel" is what our reality is. You are not going to do this without living by faith and trust. Because those counterproductive feelings do come—those little insecurities, needing to fit in and wondering how people feel about you.

If you don't get a solid understanding of what God says about you, all those insecurities will matter more than what matters most—your relationship with God.

God isn't the father who is sitting inside with arms crossed, displeased with contempt and anger; rather, he is the Father who is sprinting toward us with open arms when we come back after realizing how far we've wandered. His love is displayed in his beautifully orchestrated plan of redemption to save our lost souls. Jesus died for us and paid the price for our sin. God is always searching for us, always keeping his loving eye on us. Before we even make it to his throne, he has already met us halfway.

If you feel like it's time to stop wandering, pray this with me:

Heavenly Father, I confess that I have wandered from you. I confess to you that I was caught up in the world, and I let my selfishness reign. I repent of my ways and ask for your forgiveness, Lord. You have promised that if I confess my sins, you will wash them clean and forgive me. Please forgive me, Lord. I feel like a prodigal daughter, but I want to return to you now. Thank you for forgiving me and for remaining faithful to me, even when I became faithless and foolish toward you. Thank you for welcoming me back in your loving arms. I pray that from this day forward, I may live the life that you would have me live. Draw close to me, as I draw close to you, Lord. In Jesus' name, amen.

Reflect and Respond

1. Do you find yourself wandering? If so, how?
2. Have you accepted Christ? If so, have you felt on fire for him for a period of time and then found yourself drawing back to your old ways? What did that look like?
3. In what areas, if any, do you feel like you've wandered back into prodigal-daughter territory?
4. How does it make you feel to know that God isn't mad at you? Is that hard to believe? Is this information a relief?

Six

Your Created Value
Fearfully and Wonderfully Made

HAVE YOU EVER TAKEN YOUR time on a project that meant a lot to you? Maybe it was a song, presentation, video, or simply a drawing. Think of a moment in your life when you've had to work on something so meticulously that you poured yourself into it and made sure you did everything you could to bring it to complete perfection. And because you worked so hard on this thing, you really wanted people to like it. For me (Britt), it would have to be when I redid my grandma's kitchen.

My grandmother has always been my best friend, and to show her just how much she meant to me, I wanted to redo her kitchen DIY. Now, I couldn't buy brand-new cabinets and countertops for her, but I was able to redo everything and make it look new again. Every paint stroke I made, I did with love knowing how much it would mean to her to have a fresh and new kitchen. I was meticulous and took my time because I wanted it to be perfect. I learned how to strip the old wood off her cabinets, how to sand them properly, and how to paint each cabinet by hand in such a way that it looked like new. The labor was a privilege because I knew the end result would bless her, and it did. After all the hard work I had put into her kitchen, I couldn't imagine how I'd feel if she didn't like it or if it got ruined in some way. I had turned something old and tarnished into something new and polished for my grandma.

I'll never forget the look on her face when she saw it all finished for the first time. It made me cry. She was there for me and loved me unconditionally through my parents' divorce and throughout my thirty years of life. I felt I was returning to her just a fragment of that kind of love through my labor. Now, when I go to her house, I look at her bright, white, lovely kitchen, and I smile because the hard work was so worth it to see her blessed. I gave it my all because she gave it her all being my grandma my whole life.

If I could put that much love and effort into creating an updated kitchen for my beloved grandmother, can you imagine how intentional God was when he created you and me? How much thought and care he put into creating us?

God created the heavens and the earth. He created all the creatures on the land and in the sea, yet he looked at what he created and crowned it with us. We are God's masterpiece (Ephesians 2:10 NLT) made in his own image and likeness. God took his time on us. We are the crowning glory of God's creation. He knows the number of stars, each by name (Isaiah 40:26), and yet he knows us by name. He knows every hair on our heads (Luke 12:7). We are image bearers of God. We are fearfully and wonderfully made (Psalm 139:14).

All was well, and then the plague of sin entered the world. God's masterpiece fell into sin and was separated from him. But that isn't the end of the story. Actually, it's just the beginning. God went to great lengths to get us back.

The Gospel in a Nutshell

Each and every one of us has sinned against God. "All have sinned and fall short of the glory of God" (Romans 3:23). Scripture then goes on to say that "the wages of sin is death" (Romans 6:23). So that means when sin occurs, something must die. That's the price that must be paid. When sin entered the world, it looked like all was lost, but God made a way.

In the Old Testament, God saw fit to allow people to make a substitutionary payment. So instead of us dying, something else—usually a pure, spotless lamb—was allowed to die in our place and pay the price of our sin. We deserved death, but God made a way.

In the New Testament, we see the Lamb of God, Jesus Christ, who came to take away the sin of the world. God saw fit to allow his perfect Son to be the one-time sacrifice for all of us, forever. Jesus is perfect in every way. God gave up his precious and perfect

Son to die in our place, the greatest gift of all time. That he traded that for you and for me is unfathomable. It's unbelievable that God chose to do that. Yet he chose to do that freely, without payment from us.

Our Debt: Paid in Full

Have you ever borrowed money from someone? Most likely you have or will in the form of a credit card or mortgage loan. The total consumer debt in the United States is at $14.9 trillion, including mortgages, auto loans, credit cards and student loans.[18] We like to borrow money.

When you have a debt or owe something to someone else, you carry a heaviness because you owe someone something. In fact, the Bible says "the borrower is slave to the lender" (Proverbs 22:7). The pressure of owing money hangs over you and weighs you down. Likewise, when you pay off that debt, you have a sense of relief. You feel free, not owing anything to anybody anymore. You are no longer a slave to that debt. Likewise, God declared that your sin debt was paid in full. This means that you no longer owe the debt. The debt has been erased.

The Enemy wants to constantly remind us of our failures, our sin, and our mistakes. It's almost as though he does this to distract us from living in total freedom—debt-free. Really all he is doing is reminding us of that credit card that was paid off years ago, and that's how we need to see it. That debt has been paid. He can remind us of it all day long, but it's been paid. So, anytime he reminds you of your sin, you remind him that the debt has been paid and that his future is sealed (Revelation 20:10).

Nothing you've ever done has made God love you any less than he's always loved you. He's loved you since the beginning. And by the same token, nothing you can ever do for him could make him love you any more because he already loves you with a perfect love.

God is love.
The pressure is off.
The debt has been paid.
Your sin has been canceled.
You have been set free.
You don't have to strive to be worthy.
God knew the cost and he paid the price.

You don't have to strive to be worthy of God because the ultimate measuring stick of his love for you is Christ crucified. He so loved you that he sent his one and only Son to die in your place (John 3:16). For your sin. Paid in full.

You get to live from a place of being loved, not working for love. You get to live from a place of being affirmed by God, and his affirmation through Christ is enough. Let him strip off your identity of sin and clothe you in righteousness as his redeemed daughter. You are not your sin. You are not your past. He is calling you out of darkness and into light.

You are not damaged goods; you are brand new in Christ. Right now, in this moment, you get to start over and begin again with Jesus. We don't have to earn his mercy, just accept it as the free gift that it is. Nobody pays a high price for something that isn't valuable. You're highly treasured and precious in his sight.

Imagine How Valuable You Must Be

I (Britt) am a huge fan of garage sales, and I love a good bargain. I love finding precious, treasured items for a low cost. But I don't like it when I see an overpriced item that I know isn't worth the amount being asked.

One time I went to a garage sale near my mom's house. As I drove up, I saw it looked spectacular from the street. I walked up and down the driveway waiting for something to jump out at me. I saw a $150 price tag on a used, tarnished set of pots and pans. Then I saw a scratched wooden footstool with paisley-printed fabric priced at $70. A little farther down, I found an old rocking chair priced at $150. *Dang! This place is expensive!* In my dismay and curiosity, I pulled up the eBay app on my phone, scanned the pots and pans, and saw that the full retail value of this specific set was $100, unopened and brand new. I couldn't believe my eyes and decided to head back to my car. I thought the longer I stayed there, the greater the chances of me buying some other overpriced item.

Even after I headed home and later into the evening, I couldn't stop thinking about the price they were charging on those pots and pans. It almost felt insulting that they were attempting to charge that much. To me, they had very little value. They were very used, banged up, scratched up, and there was even a small pot missing from the set. I thought there was zero chance that anyone in their right mind would pay such a high price for that set.

At times, I have viewed myself a lot like I viewed those pots and pans—as used and worthless. Definitely worth less than the price paid for me. I wondered why God would pay the highest price for me. Me—little old me. Even if I didn't think that I was worth the blood of Jesus, the ultimate sacrifice, God says I am. And he said so by sending his Son. Sometimes I don't understand it. Sometimes I feel like I'm not valuable. I've sinned too much. I've gone too far. Did God know what a horrible deal this was? How could I possibly be worth it? But here's the kicker: my opinion doesn't change the facts. God says I am worth it. And he says you are too.

Friend, God says you are worth the blood of Jesus. Wow!

What does this mean? It means that even though we deserved death, God sent his Son, the pure and spotless Lamb of God, to die in our place. That's what the cross says about our value to God. It says we are worth the greatest gift of all time.

When we know who we are in Christ and what he did for us, understanding his sacrifice and the price he paid, we can grasp our infinite value. When we align ourselves with that truth, we can dispense with "low identity" thinking: an identity that is much less than what God says about us.

Are You Sure About Your Relationship with God?

Before we continue, if you don't know where you stand with God or if you aren't sure if you have accepted Christ, we want to take a moment for you to get sure. Salvation is God's free gift to us, but we must accept it.

So, if your heart is ready, if you are reading this and God has been pulling your heartstrings for a while now, let's seal the deal. Let's accept God's free gift.

The Bible says, "If you confess with your mouth that Jesus is Lord and believe in your heart that God raised him from the dead, you will be saved" (Romans 10:9 ESV). So it's super easy. There are two parts:

1. Say it out loud: "Jesus is Lord." To confess is to admit or state something out loud. So raise your voice and say, "Jesus is Lord."
2. Believe in your heart that God raised Jesus from the dead.

There is no magical prayer you must pray. It's more about the condition of your heart.

Some important components can be remembered with the ABCs:

Admit that you are a sinner in need of a Savior.
Believe that Jesus died for you and rose again.
Commit to live the rest of your life for him.

Does this represent your heart? If so, consider praying this example prayer below or something like it in your own words:

> *Thank you, Lord Jesus, for dying for my sins. I am a sinner and I have sinned against you. I ask for your forgiveness. I confess that you are Lord. I take you as my Lord, Jesus. I believe that God raised you from the dead. Thank you for saving me and giving me new and everlasting life. In your name, amen.*

If that is what you feel in your heart and you just prayed to accept Christ, the Bible says you are saved! It also says that the angels in heaven are rejoicing and that there is a huge party in heaven on your behalf (Luke 15:10)! We are so excited for you. Welcome to the family! Now that you are sure, let's talk about sanctification.

The Transformative Power of Sanctification

The Bible teaches us not just about the forgiveness of our sin but also the transformation of our identity through the power of *sanctification*. Salvation happens in an instant, but sanctification is a lifelong journey. You might be thinking, *Sancti-what now?* If that's you, you're in good company. The concept of being sanctified is one that can easily be misunderstood, so let's start with the basic dictionary definition of the term.

Sanctification: (noun)
1. to "sanctify" something is to set it apart for special use
2. to "sanctify" a person is to make him holy[19]

In *He Chose the Nails*, Max Lucado makes this distinction by defining "positional sanctification" as "Christ's work for us," and "progressive sanctification" as "Christ's work in us."[20] When we accept Christ and are born again, we become positionally sanctified, or "holy." God gently invites us to willingly participate in the process of our progressive sanctification or growing in spiritual maturity over time. Through the power of his Word, the purification of our hearts, and the renewing of our minds, we are transformed. Scripture encourages us, "Do not conform to the pattern of this world, but be transformed by the renewing of your mind. Then you will be able to test and approve what God's will is—his good, pleasing and perfect will" (Romans 12:2).

It's not condemnation but rather the Lord's loving-kindness that draws us to repentance (Romans 2:4). We're not strong enough to purify our own hearts. Thankfully, Jesus said that he left us a comforter through the Holy Spirit (John 14:26). Through our relationship with God, we are in communion with him—we can communicate with him, even when we don't have the words to speak (Romans 8:26).

Submitting to the lordship of Jesus Christ should be a daily event. This is a continual process of putting off the old nature and putting on the new nature. The goal is that every day we look a little more like Christ.

Selfies, side hustles, and people pleasing all offer us temporary solutions to our permanent problem. Without God, we will always be on the quest to find ourselves. It's only when we come to the end of ourselves and put our faith in Jesus that we are truly found. Our true worth is hidden in the Son and what he's done.

One Sacrifice Fits All

Just as it's critical to walk in the knowledge of our own worth to God, we must also learn to value others based on this irrevocable truth. The same blood that was spilled upon the cross to pay the cost of sin for you paid the price for us all. The blood of Jesus satisfied the ransom the gates of hell demanded. He poured it out for us all to have the opportunity to know him and be known by him. There aren't any "nobodies" in the sight of God. Therefore, we must fix our eyes on our fellow image bearers with this truth in mind.

None of us is righteous or deserving of the love of God, and yet he sent his one and only Son to be close to us. To redeem us and call us his sons and daughters. The Enemy will try to convince you to tear down others in your pursuit of wholeness. Don't fall for it. There's a reason Jesus told us that the world will know we belong to him because of the way we love one another (John 13:35). Here's the deal. We know the world will hate us (John 15:18), but that doesn't give us permission to cause conflict and stir up strife. The world doesn't need more critics creating controversy. It needs the love of Christ that we preach being practiced in the streets. The Enemy doesn't have to tear us down if we're tearing each other apart. It's an inside job, and we're the weapon of choice. We cannot be a body pitted against itself.

God instructed us to love our neighbors for a reason, and yes, that includes our annoying neighbors down the street who hold different convictions and opinions from us (Mark 12:31). We do this so the love of Christ can be poured out for the world to see through us. Demonizing people we don't understand or those we disagree with isn't loving them well. There is no partiality in the eyes of God. There is no right versus left in heaven. There is only the mighty Lion of Judah. There won't be any assigned seating based on our denominational divides. Just all of us, proclaiming, *Holy, Holy, Holy is the Lord God Almighty* (Revelation 4:8).

Our differences are what make us beautifully diverse. God is an intentional designer. He created us with differences and called us according to his marvelous purposes. Who are we to demand conformity when God clearly intended us all to function differently but in harmony within the body? We get it; different can be scary, but different doesn't always mean wrong. If the past two years of cultural chaos, political strife, denominational bickering, and polarized opinions have taught us anything, it's this: one sacrifice fits all.

Jesus loves us all unconditionally. We need to commit ourselves to loving one another the way Jesus loves us. We know it's easier said than done. But imagine the type of world we'd be living in if each of us decided to choose love over hate.

What Do You Believe About God?

What we believe about God informs how we live and what we believe about the world around us. Our beliefs inform our view of ourselves and others.

Do you believe that God cares for you? If you do, you will live from this truth. If you don't, you will live your life trying to acquire the love and affirmation of others in an endless cycle of people pleasing and rejection.

Do you believe God wants you to lead an abundant life, or do you function out of scarcity?

Do you believe God is generous? If so, you're more likely to be generous yourself.

Do you believe God is critical of you? If so, you will likely criticize yourself and others harshly.

Do you believe God is angry at you? If so, you will likely live life in hiding, attempting to dodge his judgment. And you will likely judge others in the process.

Do you believe God is gracious and gentle? If so, you will likely live your life expressing compassion and mercy toward others.

Do you believe God is your protector? If so, you will retreat to God as your refuge, and you will likely be a safe haven for others.

How you view your heavenly Father really matters. We want to make sure we are viewing him through the lens of Scripture and nothing else. He is love, joy, peace, patience, kindness, goodness, faithfulness, gentleness, and self-control—those are the "fruit" of the Spirit (Galatians 5:22–23). These attributes represent him, and he calls us to walk in them as well.

Ultimately, we pray that you now realize your created value in Christ. You were fearfully and wonderfully made. Made on purpose, for a purpose. You are the masterpiece of God's creation, and more than it all, you were worth the greatest price—Christ crucified.

Reflect and Respond

1. What habits do you need to implement on a daily basis to renew your mind?
2. Have you accepted Christ and gotten sure about your relationship with God? How has this affected you?
3. In what ways, if any, have you strived to find worth?
4. How does it make you feel to be told that you are fearfully and wonderfully made? (Psalm 139:13-14)

Seven

Undistracted, Unfiltered, and Unfettered Before God

Discovering Intimacy with God

GOD WANTS A CONNECTION WITH you and me. He desires intimacy. He isn't a robot God that gives us a to-do list and a don't-do list, then sends us off on our way. No, he desires closeness with his children.

We are reminded in John 17:3 that we are called to know him—not just to know about him or to hear about who he is from someone else. Secondhand knowledge simply won't do. We're called to know God on a deeply personal level.

Through intimacy, we have a beautiful chance to understand and know the God we worship and love and to connect our hearts to his will and align our desires with his. The more we know God through intimacy, the better we can love, serve, and worship him with our lives and the more effective we will be in the kingdom.

So, sister, let's live our lives undistracted, unfiltered, and unfettered before him. Let's dive deep into his Word to draw closer to him and fall more in love with him every day. Let's seek him when nobody else is watching.

Undistracted: Spending Time in God's Presence

Think of your closest relationship. It can be your mom or dad, brother or sister, spouse, or friend. How did you get to such a point of closeness with this person? You most likely acquired that closeness from years and years of getting to know them and spending time with them. It's really hard to consider ourselves close to someone without spending any time with them.

The first time I (Britt) ever experienced God's presence, I could almost tangibly reach out and touch it. It was that powerful. I was at a really, really low point in my life. I was coming out of a very unhealthy relationship full of sin, and I was all alone on New Year's Eve. My boyfriend at the time had ditched me to party with some girls, which left me feeling unlovable and worthless. My mom was overseas for work, and the rest of my family had other plans that night. So I was alone. Ushering in the new year, I sat in the dark in my living room as I watched the ball drop on the TV. I felt so alone, low, and worthless. What had become of me? I kept asking myself this as I continued to battle with suicidal thoughts.

Then I heard a still, small voice prompt me to pray in the midst of my despair. There I sat, cross-legged on the couch with a broken heart, shaky hands, and tears streaming down my face. "Lord, please give me peace." I kept asking him over and over again. "Please give me peace, God." I hadn't known the feeling of peace in my entire life—the true peace that only he can give.

As I sat there, undoing my heart before him, it was as if I could see his light surrounding me in that dark living room. It was as though myriads of sparkling lights were all around me, so bright and dazzling I couldn't help but gaze in wonder. The light was exposing every dark thing in my life that was binding me in chains, and all that was left once those chains hit the ground was the tangible presence of God surrounding me. His love felt like a weighted blanket that covered over me, yet it somehow made me feel as light as a feather. That's really the best way I can explain it.

I had never experienced anything like that before in my entire life. He met me in the pit of my despair. He came to me in my brokenness and surrounded me with his love. He gave me the peace I had so desperately begged him for. I was bare before him, exposed, but in a good way. I was safe in his embrace. I knew he saw me; he saw my hurt and my pain and kissed it with his love and his peace. I had never felt so loved. I had never experienced this peace that truly surpassed understanding (Philippians 4:7). I sat there, totally present in the moment. No distractions. Just me and my heavenly Father. Basking in his perfect and complete love. In his presence I felt whole.

It's amazing how God gave us five senses to take in his

creation around us. We look around and see people, art, architecture, animals, flowers, nature. But with all God has allowed us to see, hear, feel, taste, and smell, he has chosen to not make himself visible to us. Even in that moment on New Year's Eve, when I felt so close to his beating heart, wrapped in his arms of perfect peace and love, I still could not see him. But I didn't need to see him to know that he was there. I didn't need visible proof of his love. I felt it in my spirit as I cried out to him.

You see, we can experience closeness with God without visibly seeing him. We don't need to see him to spend time with him. Every single one of our senses shows us proof every day that he is there. When we see his beautiful creation around us. When we hear the Holy Spirit speaking to us through Scripture. When we feel the peace he gives us in our despair. He is truly all around us, closer than our very breath.

Whether we're new Christians or mature in our faith, spending time with our Creator is crucial for every believer's walk. In that secret place with him, we are strengthened, equipped, refined, and purified. Seek him when nobody's looking.

Knowing our true identity in Christ begins with time spent in his Word and in prayer. I love the popular sermon quote: "When asked, 'What is more important: prayer or reading the Bible?' I ask, 'What is more important; breathing in or breathing out?'" You truly cannot have one without the other. Both are equally important when it comes to spending time with God.

Reading the Word of God ignites the strongest joy your soul

will ever experience while at the same time cutting through the lies and deception that the Enemy has spoken.

> The Word of God is alive and active. Sharper than any double-edged sword, it penetrates even to dividing soul and spirit, joints and marrow; it judges the thoughts and attitudes of the heart. Nothing in all creation is hidden from God's sight. Everything is uncovered and laid bare before the eyes of him to whom we must give account. (Hebrews 4:12–13)

You see, how can we know who we are in him if we don't truly know him? And what does it really take to know God? We find out who God is by spending time with him. And we spend time with him by reading his Word and communicating with him in prayer. This ensures that we are knowing him for ourselves and seeking after him. Not just knowing about him through what people tell us but knowing him intimately. Spending time in his presence and seeing him for ourselves, not through the lens of others.

I could tell you all day long who God is to me, but until you experience him on your own you won't truly know him. God desires us to know him and be known by him. This is why spending time with God is essential.

I often get asked what it looks like to spend time with God, and I want to start out by first saying that Jesus set the perfect example for us by frequently withdrawing to the wilderness to pray and talk with the Father. The Bible says, "Jesus often withdrew to lonely places and prayed" (Luke 5:16).

Jesus withdrew from everything around him and understood the importance of being quiet and still before his Father. He turned off every distraction by going into deserted places to be inhabited by God's voice, power, and will.

What distractions do you need to turn off or put aside to press into God's presence? That's why we say to seek him when nobody else is watching, friend. It's in those quiet, still, intimate moments that something beautiful is built.

Unfiltered: Being Bare Before God

I (Britt) think we can all relate to feeling seen but not truly known, especially when we're misunderstood and misrepresented. I have a vivid memory of a time in high school when this happened to me. I was in eleventh grade. The shrill noise of the bell rang, and I stood up from my desk and hurried to grab my books from my locker. I needed to get to study hall swiftly so I wasn't tardy. I was always tardy to my classes because I was new to this school and was still learning the layout.

As I got to study hall, breathless from hurrying, a girl who I didn't even know aggressively approached me. I looked behind me and side to side trying to see if she was walking toward someone else. Lo and behold, it was me she was darting at with an angry scowl on her face. I was so confused because I had never met her before and, in that split second of her approach, didn't understand why she would be so angry with me. I had butterflies of embarrassment in my stomach as she stomped her feet closer to me.

She then shoved me back, shouting, "Were you the one flirting with my boyfriend?!" Followed by all sorts of other insults and threats that if I kept talking to her boyfriend, I'd get my butt kicked by her and her friends.

I, of course, defended myself and told her I didn't know what she was referring to. Well, it turns out, her boyfriend's locker was right next to mine. Again, I had no idea because I was new. How would I know who was dating whom at that time? I remembered a brief conversation I had with some guy asking him about the location of one of my classes. Of course someone saw and spread a rumor that I was flirting with him. Gotta love high school. A five-second conversation turned into a flirtatious interaction according to the one spreading the rumor. Not exactly the "Welcome to your new school!" I was hoping for.

I felt an ache in the pit of my stomach when I returned home that day from school. It was day ten in my new school, and people already hated me for something I hadn't done. They didn't even know me, but I had been seen talking to the wrong person and shamed for it.

We've all had moments when we've been *seen* by others but not truly *known*.

We enjoy being seen, admired, and affirmed, but at what cost? We cannot rely on our phones to make us feel seen and known. We cannot rely on people to fulfill that desire to be seen and known. But that desire doesn't disappear. It is deeply woven within the fiber of our beings. It's a part of God's highly intelligent and intricate design. The purpose of that longing is to be seen and known by him. God not only created us to be known by him but also desires for us to see him in every sunset, to search his Word, and to know his heart. The filters through which we view ourselves and others are skewed, but God can see through it all.

God isn't intimidated by our humanity. When we bare our souls before him, he does not recoil. Nothing is hidden from him (Hebrews 4:13). He doesn't assume the worst about what he sees and then spread a rumor about us. No, he knows us.

And those bruised, battered, and blemished areas of our stories are the very same ruins God wants to redeem and restore. Only when we can recognize and reconcile with our pasts can we peel back the Band-Aids we've placed on wounds that only he can heal.

Rest assured that if there's anyone you can stand bare and vulnerable in front of, it's Jesus.

> He sees you, and he knows you.
> He knows every fiber of your being (Psalm
>   139:1, 13)
>   down to the very number of hair strands on
>   your head. (Luke 12:7)
> He knows every detail about you,
>   every broken fragment,
>   every mistake you've made.
> Yet he loves you the same.

To be *seen by God* is to be noticed and looked upon. He is *El Roi*, the God who sees us. To be *known by God* is to be fully understood, fully accepted, fully loved, and fully embraced as we are.

What a joy it is to be seen and known by God! We don't have to strive for or obtain perfection around him. We can be completely unfiltered in his presence. We can unashamedly come before him, bare, and be loved by him all the same.

The concept of being seen and known by God might be a hard one for some of us to fully comprehend. I (Cass) have personally had difficulty wrapping my head around the fact that God sees me when circumstances in my life have often led me to believe that the opposite must be true. There's a story in the Bible I cling to that has helped me understand how, no matter the plights of my life, I am in fact seen and know by God. Let's talk about Hagar.

Hagar Was Seen and Known by God

Hagar was a slave in a land that was not her own. A foreigner, used, rejected, and discarded once her usefulness expired. A pawn in her masters' attempt to fulfill a divine promise on their own terms. A runaway bound to a man she did not choose, through circumstances beyond her control. Knocked up, despised, and desperate to escape her situation, she ran—but she could not outrun her problems.

Alone in the wilderness, Hagar encountered God at a well. He called her by name and instructed her to return to her masters, but he also offered her a promise: "I will increase your descendants so much that they will be too numerous to count" (Genesis 16:10). In that moment Hagar named the Lord *El Roi*, "the One who sees me" (Genesis 16:13). She is the first person in Bible history to give a name to God. A woman, a slave, and an abused runaway. Yet he knew her by name, and she gave him a name, *El Roi*.

Several years later, Hagar and her child were cast out by her masters, and she found herself in the wilderness yet again. She was banished into the desert. I (Cass) imagine her feet scorched by the heat of the sand as beads of sweat drip down her face. Out of options and without hope, she laid her young son down in a bush to die—but that was not the end of their story! Once again, God intervened. He saw their desperation and heard their cries for help. "Lift the boy up and take him by the hand, for I will make him into a great nation" (Genesis 21:18).

God revealed something she had not seen before. Blinded by her grief, somehow she'd missed it! She could not see the well that would save their lives until the water she carried ran dry. But God saw her.

How often is that our story? How often do we wait until we're totally out of options before we look to him?! This is where I slowly raise my hand. It's me, sis. Maybe it's you too.

Have you ever found yourself in circumstances beyond your control? Battered, bruised, and broken beyond repair? Oppressed, rejected, and feeling utterly defeated? Join the club, sister. I've got good news!

Our God is the God who *sees* you, he *hears* you, and he *knows* you by name!

He is *El Roi*, the God who sees.

We Are Seen and Known by God

Let's pause for a moment of brutal honesty. We know that it's hard to be totally bare before God. It requires a level of honesty with ourselves that can often be difficult to access.

Much like Hagar, there are ways in which I (Cass) have tried to run away from home, particularly when it comes to addressing the wounds of my childhood. When the healing process feels too painful, I have a tendency to opt out and pro-Cass-tinate, which only delays the process of healing. Maybe you can relate.

I was in one of those opt-out zones recently when my husband and I took our three children to visit my extended family in the lakeside city where I spent most of my childhood. It was the first time I'd been back in many years.

For me, this city wasn't just a geographical place; it was a jagged emotional scar. Just being there was like brushing up against a wound that caused me to wince and cry out in pain—a pain I very much preferred to ignore and bury so I wouldn't have to deal with it.

But there was no ignoring the pain on this trip. As we crossed the state line, all the memories and emotions I'd buried rushed over me. Warm tears rolled down my cheeks, and I had no choice but to become vulnerable with God, with my husband, and with myself. I had to allow myself to be unfiltered and bare. And God saw me in my pain. *El Roi* knew I needed to go there, and he received me with tenderness upon arrival.

After years of burying my pain and living with a fortified heart, I had almost given up hope that anything could be different for me—that there could be healing in my life and relationships. I was in danger of becoming emotionally closed off and writing off my relationships as broken beyond repair.

But now I felt a flicker of hope ignite within me, and I dared to believe that total healing really could be possible for me. And it happened! I experienced the first signs of hope becoming a reality during our visit there. Are there areas of my story that still ache? Yes, of course. But I no longer feel compelled to run away from them. Instead, I want to be seen and known and healed by God.

The beautiful irony about writing a book on the topic of knowing our worth and identity in Christ is that, through the conviction of the Holy Spirit, I've had to confront the formative years of my life that led me to believe I was worthless. I've had to come face-to-face with the reality of my own lived experiences and process that pain in real time with the guidance of wise counsel and the support of my loving husband. I've had to offer apologies for my poor responses to trauma triggers, repent, and take full responsibility for my actions. I've had to do some honest inward reflection and participate in the messy work of uprooting dysfunctional behaviors and challenging false beliefs. In daring to become bare before God, I experienced decades of brokenness repaired.

Here's what I want you to take away from this personal story: *running from our pain and concealing our wounds from God doesn't protect us; it hinders the healing our hearts yearn for.* Dear friend, take it from me: ignoring your pain doesn't make you immune to it but just makes you numb to it.

Have you ever had your foot fall asleep? It gets kind of tingly, but a loss of sensation doesn't mean the loss of a limb. Your foot is still there; it just feels numb. The same can be said of our emotional pain. Our refusal to address the wounds life has left us doesn't stop the pain from affecting us. Even when you're afraid to touch the source of your despair, God is already there, tenderly waiting for you to arrive and allow him to tend to your wounds.

Being bare before God means baring our souls before him and trusting him not to betray us. It's difficult to come to that level of vulnerability if you've suffered at the hands of those you should have been able to trust, but God isn't like us. His ways are not our ways, and he truly is trustworthy.

What I'm learning is that sometimes, when we're convinced a chapter is closed, God isn't finished writing our stories. He's intentional with his timing and handles our hearts with delicate care. I'm grateful God didn't allow my pain to be the main character of my story.

I'm so glad that my story didn't stop there. I'm thankful that I can now see those who I once viewed as the villains of my story with compassion and empathy because the inconvenient truth is this: *they're a lot like me.* Wounded and hurting people, trying their best to process their pain. Desperate hearts in need of the same unconditional love and mercy I received through the cross. Their pain doesn't excuse their behavior, but it does give me the ability to forgive them.

Returning to the ruins of my past gave me the ability to access my damage and allow God to build something totally new. As I revisited places that once held painful memories, it was like reclaiming enemy ground. What was once broken was now being restored. What I once was too afraid to touch no longer holds the power to harm me.

When we think of God healing our wounds, we want to believe it's going to happen all at once. Sometimes it does. But I'm slowly learning that often the healing comes one piece at a time through intimacy with God. Slowly he's mending my heart one fragment at a time. I'm learning to embrace the process of my healing. It's gentle and it's intentional. One wound at a time. "He heals the brokenhearted and binds up their wounds" (Psalm 147:3).

Friend, be patient with yourself. Healing one wound at a time is still healing.

Unfettered: Breaking Chains and Living Free

Chains are an obvious symbol of imprisonment. In physical terms, they restrict and entrap us, holding us down and keeping us in a state of captivity. In spiritual terms they do more or less the same. Spiritual chains keep us in bondage, enslaved to whatever is holding us prisoner. This can be a variety of things—sin, sickness, addiction, failure to forgive, emotional pain.

The danger of living in bondage is that our chains inhibit and restrict us from growing and maturing spiritually. Some of us may not even realize we're living chained up and in bondage. The best way to identify what chains we are being bound by is to look at our walk with Christ. Are we feeling held back from getting closer to him and becoming more like him? Do we have any unconfessed sin in our lives that keep us in shame? Do our hearts feel hardened in certain areas and we don't understand why?

If the answer is yes, the good news is that Jesus comes to destroy the chains that bind us. I love how the psalmist described the Lord's power to set us free:

> Then they cried to the LORD in their trouble,
>   and he saved them from their distress.
> He brought them out of darkness, the utter
>   darkness,
>   and broke away their chains.
> Let them give thanks to the LORD for his unfailing
>   love
>   and his wonderful deeds for mankind,
> for he breaks down gates of bronze
>   and cuts through bars of iron.
> (Psalm 107:13–16)

If you find yourself in trouble, God can rescue you. There's no bondage he can't break.

I (Britt) have experienced the burden of carrying chains that have restricted me in life. Before I entered the beauty industry, I was a fitness trainer. I was twenty-three, newly married, and didn't really know what I wanted to do with my life because I dropped out of college prior to our wedding. Before my husband and I got married, I worked out *a lot*. I practically lived at the gym, and dry shampoo was my best friend. I was obsessed with the "fit" lifestyle and found myself in "sweating for the wedding" mode on a daily basis.

So, naturally, when we got married, I thought, *Why not pursue a career as a fitness trainer since I am so engulfed in that culture anyway?* The problem for me wasn't necessarily the career choice; I know and respect many fitness trainers who help people attain their goals to become healthier. My issue was that it became an addiction for me.

I was addicted to results, and I would experience paralyzing fear if I gained a couple of pounds or saw something in the mirror that I didn't like. It was like I had a chisel in my hands and couldn't stop striking it on my body to the point where there was nothing left of me but bones. I was never happy or satisfied, and because I wasn't, I'd continue to push myself harder and punish my body more and more for not being perfect. I got stuck in a vicious cycle of working out excessively and eating basically nothing if I saw that number on the scale go up or didn't see the results I was demanding of my body.

I look back now and feel sadness that I treated my body this way. I was bound in the chains of anorexia and body dysmorphia without even realizing I was being held captive.

I'm five feet six and not a petite person. I've always had an athletic yet curvier build. So you can imagine that at five feet six, weighing 117 pounds, I was pretty thin. I hated when people would tell me I was too skinny because when I looked in the mirror, I still saw an overweight person. I felt trapped in my own body that I hated. I so badly wanted to love and accept myself as I was, but it was never enough. I was never enough. I was in chains and bondage, and instead of going to the Lord to set me free, I attempted to take matters into my own hands first.

I stopped working out, stopped dieting, and just thought eliminating it all from the equation would solve the problem entirely. Wrong. I slapped a Band-Aid on the root of the problem and then I went from one extreme to the other. From over-restricting to overeating. One hundred pounds of weight gain later, I was depressed and absolutely disgusted with myself that I had let myself go. That drove me further into self-loathing—more than ever.

Why was I so obsessed with my body? Why couldn't I just get it right? I couldn't feel content at my thinnest, and I hated myself even more at my heaviest. I either punished my body by over-restricting or tried to mask the pain by overeating. None of it worked, and I felt so helpless. I'm not kidding; it took me years to break out of this bondage because I kept trying to control my situation and fix it instead of just surrendering to the Lord in it. I had gone through medical weight loss programs, started and then failed at keto about twenty times, and just couldn't lose the weight I had gained. Failure became a familiar friend that visited me often.

Finally, I reached a point of total exhaustion. I was tired of living this way. So I sought the Lord's guidance, and he delivered me from this bondage in my life. I spent hours in his presence, taking my pain to his throne. Freedom came almost immediately for me. All those years I tried to control my situation, and it was as though he was waiting for me there, waiting for me to take his hand and trust him in my brokenness. He was so gentle with me and such a loving Father to guide me through something that I had no idea how to get out of.

I'll never forget the moment I felt him speak to me that the weight gain was a blessing in disguise because it brought me closer to him. My heart sank into my chest because I couldn't imagine how he could use something I felt so terrible about for his glory. It was as though I had to be stripped to the bare bones of myself, to the point where I couldn't rely on my looks to feel worthy, and only then was I able to really grasp who I was in him.

I won't lie to you or sugarcoat anything: the Enemy still tempts me with these feelings of hating and obsessing over my body every day. I have to actively speak truth into those lies every single day. It's like maintaining a healthy, fruit-producing garden. You have to tend to it and water it daily. You can't neglect it and expect it to not grow weeds. The same thing goes with our minds. You're not always going to feel free, but that's why the Bible says to walk by faith and to renew your mind (Romans 12:2). We have to cling to the Word of God and his truth every day. We can't afford not to. Remember, "We live by faith, not by sight" (2 Corinthians 5:7).

Know this, friend: just because the temptation is there doesn't mean you haven't found freedom from it. The Enemy loves to deceive us and get us thinking we're not really free when Jesus says that the person he sets free is free indeed (John 8:36).

Don't allow yourself to accept that your feelings are always speaking the truth to you. God gave us our feelings, yes, but remember the first trick the Enemy used in the garden was to sow doubt into Eve's mind—a.k.a. her feelings. We're supposed to trust God before we trust our feelings. The spirit is willing, but the flesh is weak (Matthew 26:41). Feelings come and go. They're fleeting. There are a million things that can affect how we feel. God is our anchor and our firm strength and keeps us grounded because *he* is not fleeting.

He is steady. He is constant. He is trustworthy. God loves you far too much to leave you in bondage. He wants us to know how he built us too—and how we can change.

Wired to Change

Have you ever heard the saying, "You're just wired that way"? Essentially this saying means that our brains are hardwired to think, feel, and act a certain way based on what behaviors we partake in. So when we learn anything, whether it's a new language, a new sport, a new instrument, we need to strengthen the neural pathways in the brain to learn these new activities.

Think about driving a car. Do you remember going through driver's training and having to learn all the aspects on how to operate a vehicle? How to parallel park, use your turn signal, change lanes safely—all these little things we probably don't even think about now when we get in the car and drive, we once had to learn and create new neural pathways in the brains for. What was so foreign to us in the beginning became so easy that we don't even have to think about it anymore.

When I (Britt) was sixteen and driving for the first time, I was always so nervous because I didn't feel confident yet. I felt overwhelmed by all the steps I had to remember just to get from point A to point B. My dad encouraged me and told me that one day it would be as easy as breathing and I wouldn't have to think about every little action. He was so right! Fifteen years later, I just get in the car and go without thinking through the steps. The "driving" neural pathway is so ingrained in my brain that getting in my car to drive is now second nature.

What's even more interesting about these new neural pathways is that, just like you can create them, you can get rid of old ones and replace them with new and healthier ones. So when you want to create a better habit of waking up early in the morning instead of snoozing, it might take time, but eventually your brain and body will adjust, and it gets easier and easier. So you're replacing sleeping in with getting up early. I find it so fascinating how God created us so intelligently and so intricately.

A neural pathway can create a habit of sin, but it can also create a habit of pursuing God every day and becoming more and more like Christ. When we repeat a sin over and over again, the beauty of finding freedom in Jesus doesn't just happen spiritually or emotionally; there is a physical change in the brain when we decide to choose Jesus over partaking in sin.

So instead of falling into the temptation to watch something we shouldn't be watching when we are alone at night, we can replace that with reading his Word and doing something that honors him. Over time, our brains make it physically easier to repent and abide in him. As we continue to seek him, we will find him and know him.

Developing Intimacy with God

The art of abiding in God is developed through daily intimacy with him. Just like our earthly relationships require time to establish intimacy, so it is with our relationship with God. Like insecurity, intimacy is a learned practice that we must participate in daily. We have the promise that when we seek him, our heavenly Father is faithful to be found (Jeremiah 29:13), and when we draw close to him, he will always draw close to us (James 4:8).

Here are three simple ways we can develop a deeply intimate relationship with God:

1. *Become undistracted:* We must remove anything that can create a wedge between us and God. It's time to ditch distractions.
2. *Become unfiltered:* We are seen and known by God. It's time to come out of hiding and dare to become bare before God.
3. *Become unfettered:* By surrendering our struggles to Christ, we can find freedom. It's time to shake off the chains that bind us.

When we live our lives undistracted, unfiltered, and un-fettered, we can walk in the fullness of intimacy that God intends for us. Today is a good day to begin the life-altering practice of fostering intimacy with God.

Reflect and Respond

1. Do you struggle to spend time with God? If so, what distractions do you need to turn off or put aside to prioritize seeking God's presence?
2. What emotion stirs up within you when you think about the concept of being seen and known by God?
3. Was there a part of Hagar's story that you person-ally resonated with? If so, what did you resonate with and why?
4. Are you carrying the burden of bondage in your life? If so, what chains are you trusting Jesus to break off today?

Eight

Fertile Soil and a Firm Foundation

Why It's Important to Be Rooted and Grounded

RECENTLY, I (BRITT) HAVE GOTTEN really into buying houseplants and caring for them. The first houseplant I ever bought for my home was a fiddle-leaf fig. I was at a greenhouse with my grandma when I saw this gorgeous plant, and I had to have it. It was so full and healthy. The leaves were a glistening, dark green, and I already had the perfect spot for it at home. Sixty-five dollars later, it was in my car on its way to its new home. I was so excited!

139

When I brought my new plant home, I put it in the corner of my living room and just thought it was like any other plant—you water it a couple of times a week and it's good to go. Wrong. Two weeks later, the leaves started turning brown and crunchy. When I went to water it, the water would just pass by the soil; it didn't look like the roots were even absorbing anything. The soil had gone dry, and there were little bugs munching on the leaves. What had I done wrong?!

I went on Facebook and added myself to every houseplant group I could find to seek some answers. I kept seeing people refer to the fiddle-leaf fig as the "fickle-leaf fig" because this plant is so finicky about its care. *Ugh.* I had no clue what I had gotten myself into. I didn't want my plant to die, but it didn't look like it was doing too good. I tried everything. I tried moving it, I tried watering it more. But it somehow just kept getting worse.

I did some more research and found out that my plant required a very specific care plan to keep it healthy. This picky plant needed a warm, humid environment, a *perfect* amount of water, with plenty of light but not *too* much light. It also couldn't sit by air vents or spots in the house that were drafty. It needed to be directly in front of or close to a southern- or western-facing window. The list went on and on.

What a high-maintenance plant I had bought! But I wasn't ready to give up just yet. I kept fighting and fighting to keep my plant alive. Despite my efforts, though, it didn't make it. Seeing it sit at the end of our driveway for the garbage truck to scoop it up made me feel so defeated. I vowed from that day on to make sure I knew how to care for each one of my houseplants before I bought them because it broke my heart to see that fiddle-leaf fig not make it.

Much like my poor fiddle-leaf fig, our relationship with Christ needs to be tended to with the utmost care. We need to allow Christ to till and purify the soil in our hearts to promote growth, healing, and strength in our walk with him. We need to allow his light to come in and shine on the areas in our lives that keep us from him. We can't expect to neglect the soil and have the growth that we desire.

Becoming Fertile Soil

I (Britt) love that Jesus spoke in parables and often used God's beautiful creation to illustrate a message he was trying to convey. One of my favorites is the parable of the sower. It could have just as easily been called the "parable of the soils" because it focuses on four different kinds of soil. Jesus explained what each kind of soil represents:

> When anyone hears the message about the kingdom and does not understand it, the evil one comes and snatches away what was sown in their heart. This is the seed sown along the path. The seed falling on rocky ground refers to someone who hears the word and at once receives it with joy. But since they have no root, they last only a short time. When trouble or persecution comes because of the word, they quickly fall away. The seed falling among the thorns refers to someone who hears the word,

but the worries of this life and the deceitfulness of wealth choke the word, making it unfruitful. But the seed falling on good soil refers to someone who hears the word and understands it. This is the one who produces a crop, yielding a hundred, sixty or thirty times what was sown. (Matthew 13:19–23)

Quick summary:

- The *sower* is the Lord.
- The *seed* is the Word of God.
- The *hard path/soil* represents those who are hardened by sin.
- The *rocky soil* refers to those who have joyfully received the Word but lack roots, so they quickly fall away.
- The *thorny soil* is the person who loves God's Word but never fully surrenders because they are too worried about worldly things.
- The *good soil* represents those who hear the Word, understand it, apply it, and allow the Word to transform them and produce great fruit.

What soil best represents you currently? I say *currently* because no matter what soil you are right now, you aren't there permanently. Millions of people all over the world love personality tests, questionnaires, self-assessments, learning about tendencies, and so forth. In some ways, I have resisted many of the popular ones because I don't like the idea of being put in a box. Well, in this case, you always get to choose what type of soil you are.

Each day we choose, with our free will, what type of soil we will be. Full disclosure: some days I wake up on the wrong side of the bed because I've allowed the smaller things in life to matter more than what matters most. In those moments, I'm thorny soil. Other times I'm locked in and feel fully connected to God. I'm living the Word actively and wanting to change the world for him. In those moments, I'm the good soil.

I don't know about you, but I don't want to quickly fall away at the first sign of trouble. The Word of God is meant to strengthen you and help you stand during life's twists and turns. I want to grow roots that are deep, mature, and unbreakable. So when the storms of life come, and they will, nothing will shake me. The apostle James wrote, "Do not merely listen to the word, and so deceive yourselves. Do what it says" (James 1:22). But how do we do that? How do we level up our soil?

The Thankful Morning Routine

Start your day off right by allowing your first waking moments to be thankful prayer and praise to God. Thank him for another day of life. Before you grab your phone and your feet hit the floor, talk to him. Thank him for all he has done and for the day to come. Thankfulness has a way of kicking other feelings to the curb— like fear, anxiety, and anger. It's hard to be fearful and thankful at the same time.

Here are some quick morning habits that can help you level up your soil. Have a quiet time with God every day:

- Take five minutes to list all the things you are thankful for.
- Read the Bible—your physical Bible or the YouVersion Bible app (it's free).
- Ask God for his help—tell him your cares, concerns, and worries.
- Listen to worship music. Worshipping God sets the frequency of your heart toward him.

This entire routine takes only twenty minutes if you spend five minutes on each part, or you can adjust it if you have more time. If you add this to your mornings, it can change your life and relationship with God (and others). I (Britt) say others because it's hard to fight with someone after you have spent time with the King of glory. Quiet, dedicated time with God has a way of softening hearts.

Regardless of what type of soil you are at this moment, you can move toward becoming the good soil. Submit yourself to God, and he will make the soil of your heart fertile, ready to produce bountiful fruit in your life.

Christ Is Our Firm Foundation

I (Britt) really enjoy reading books to my daughter, Ariana. Recently we read the childhood classic called *The Three Little Pigs*. If you're anything like me, you need a good memory refresher of this story.

There were three little pigs who each built a house and a wolf who was looking to make a meal out of the pigs. The first two pigs didn't take very much time building their houses, which is why they inevitably regretted their lack of resourcefulness.

The first and oldest pig built his house from straw. The second of the three little pigs built his house from sticks. The final of the three little pigs, and the last surviving one, built his house with bricks. When the hungry wolf came strolling around looking for a meal out of these pigs, each one of them took refuge in their own house.

If you remember, the first two pigs' houses didn't make it because their foundations and walls were built with sticks and straw. They couldn't withstand the wolf huffing and puffing to blow their house down. Then the wolf came in to eat them up.

The last pig survived because he was protected by his house built from bricks. His house couldn't be blown down by the wolf, and so the wolf left, and the pig survived. Of course, there are other renditions of this story where all the pigs survive because the other two hid out in the stronger house.

The question I'm asking is this: What is your "house" made of? Are you using straw, sticks, and sand? Or are you using Christ as your cornerstone and building your house upon him—our solid rock?

The truth is, we're not worrying about *if* the wolf comes but *when* he will come. And by wolf I mean the Enemy of our souls. Remember, he is a thief who comes to devour, kill, and destroy

(John 10:10). But he cannot destroy those who are in Christ Jesus. When we lay our foundation on Christ, we are building our houses on a rock that can withstand every evil thrown at it. The Enemy will always be after what God is building in our lives. He doesn't want us to be firm in who we are in Christ because then we'll be untouchable.

What are the wolves in your life?

What is your house built upon?

For me, the wolf that has been attacking me is fear. Since the day I gave birth to my daughter, I have struggled with postpartum depression and anxiety. I had never battled anxiety before, and now it's something I bring before God daily. To the best of my ability, I try to follow the apostle Paul's admonition:

> Do not be anxious about anything, but in every situation, by prayer and petition, with thanksgiving, present your requests to God. And the peace of God, which transcends all understanding, will guard your hearts and your minds in Christ Jesus. (Philippians 4:6–7)

I'm not going to write this as if I've mastered fear in my life because, as a new mother, it looks for me daily. There have been days I've felt so tormented by worry and anxiety regarding my daughter's health that I've spiraled into a frenzy of fear. My husband, Ryan, has found me on my bedroom floor crying because of how irrationally afraid I am of losing my daughter to something awful. Some days anxiety has tried to overtake me, but by God's grace, it hasn't succeeded.

Fear often disguises itself in those innocent what-if scenarios that my brain sifts through. One time when I talked to Ryan about it, asking him for prayer, he encouraged my heart by telling me this: "Fear robs you of the joy in the here and now." Fear of the future robs you of the joy of today. You can't be present in the moment when your mind is worried about the future. Fear paralyzes you and makes you feel as if you are walking around in a horror movie that never ends. If you see everything from the lens of those what-if scenarios rather than cultivating thankfulness, it's so easy to get stuck in a hamster wheel of anxiety.

But there is hope. Jesus calls us to live in the here and now. Jesus said, "Do not worry about tomorrow, for tomorrow will worry about itself. Each day has enough trouble of its own" (Matthew 6:34). We can choose to shorten our view. I don't know about you, but if I pull back too far in my field of view and see everything I have on my plate as a wife, mother, leader, author, friend, sister, and more, it can get overwhelming. That's why shortening my view has really helped.

My grandmother shared some wisdom with me that has changed my outlook. She said: "If this week is too big, look at today. If today is too big, look at the hour. If the hour is too big, look at the minute. Focus on the next right step." That has helped me more than I can convey. I pray it helps you as well.

As many times as the Enemy has attempted to use his fear

tactics on me, he does not prevail. Will you stand firm with me in this declaration?

- My "house" is strong. (Isaiah 32:18)
- My foundation is laid upon Christ. (Matthew 7:24–25)
- When the big bad wolf comes, I will stand firm. (Psalm 56:3)
- I will live in the moment and be present. (Matthew 6:34)
- I have no fear of tomorrow. (Proverbs 31:25)
- My future is secure. (Jeremiah 29:11)
- No weapon formed against me will prosper. (Isaiah 54:17)
- I am rooted in truth and grounded in God's love. (Ephesians 3:17–19)
- There is nothing I cannot face because God is with me. (Romans 8:31)

Make this a daily declaration if needed. Remind yourself of the truth you stand in. Remember this verse: "There is no fear in love. But perfect love drives out fear, because fear has to do with punishment. The one who fears is not made perfect in love" (1 John 4:18).

God is love, and he has called us to love. There is no fear in love, and fear has no chance against thankfulness. When we're secure in Christ, we're building upon a firm foundation, not a house of straw on a wobbly table where one swift breeze makes them crumble. When we're secure in Christ, we're building our houses on a rock and not on sand (Matthew 7:24).

Damage Control

It was an ordinary day when I (Cass) stepped into our master bedroom barefoot and felt the water seeping through the cracks of our wood floor. You never expect something like this to happen, but when it does, all you can do is pull up all the wooden planks and assess the damage. Here's the thing: This happened months ago. Time has passed. A pandemic flipped our world upside down, and our master bedroom remains the bane of my existence. What once was my refuge has become a snare.

I'm the type of person who is deeply affected by my environment. The scent of a fragranced candle, the color of the paint on the walls, and the texture of the rug underneath my feet—all these things contribute to my general mood and well-being. Maybe I'm weird. Or maybe you can totally relate . . . Either way, the clutter of my unfinished and damaged bedroom sometimes feels suffocating. I swiftly shut the door behind me as soon as I finish getting dressed most mornings.

As if leaving the door shut will somehow absolve me from assessing the chaos and repairing the disarray. In my attempt to avoid the damage, I am allowing it to remain. It is slowly chipping away at me.

Ironically, I've mismanaged my emotions in a similar fashion. When things become overwhelming, I have an unhealthy tendency to shut the door of my heart and post a Do Not Enter sign. As if I were capable of keeping God out of my dysfunctional heart.

Here's the thing about unfelt damage: *it remains unrepaired.*

God isn't intimidated by our messes, and he certainly isn't surprised by them. He's not a judgy house guest who cringes at a peek inside the messy interior of our lives. He is the type of friend who rolls up his sleeves and grabs the trash bags. He isn't willing to leave our pain and destruction undealt with. He insists on rebuilding the ruins of our lives where others have carelessly torn us down. But we have to be willing participants in our healing process.

Take comfort in this: there is nothing God's careful hand cannot repair if we open the door and let him in.

Whether you've established the wrong foundation or the foundation you did have got flooded and ruined or the soil of your heart isn't conducive to healthy growth—God can repair what has been broken, and he can heal what has been torn.

In him, you're standing on fertile ground.

In him, your foundation is untouchable, unmatched, and unequivocally stronger than the wolves that try to tear it down.

I'm not sure who else needs to hear this, but I definitely need to hear this every day! Your mission is where your feet are. Where you are *right now*—it matters. It's only insignificant if you believe it is. What you're doing now, in the quiet, is making a profound impact in unseen ways. The ripple of your obedience today will burst forth into waves that splash into countless lives. Focus on taking one step at a time.

Press your bare feet into the grass and notice the way the ground feels as you take another step forward. Plant your feet firmly in the space God has placed you. Keep allowing Christ to build the foundation laid before you. It matters.

Reflect and Respond

1. What kind of soil best represents you today? What would it take to move you closer to the good soil more often?
2. What wolves in your life are you currently dealing with?
3. What would it take for you to take your mornings back and incorporate the thankful morning routine?
4. Have you ever placed a Do Not Enter sign on the door of your heart? Have you ever worried that your foundation is damaged beyond repair? If so, how has this chapter affected you?

Nine

Circumstances Change
Your Identity in Christ Remains the Same

WE'VE ALL HAD THE OCCASIONAL bad day, and for some reason—I (Britt) am not sure why—on those days it seems like everything keeps adding up to prove the classic statement: "When it rains, it pours!" You know what I mean?

Like when you wake up to get ready for the day, pour your cup of coffee, and spill it all over the counter. *Ugh. I guess this is how today is going to go.* Then literally everything after that initial coffee spill seems almost comical because everything seems to go wrong. Hitting every red light on your way to work, stepping on gum on your way in your work building, getting yelled at by your boss right when you walk through the doors, and it goes on! We've all had days like these—where we feel defeated by our circumstances.

I swear—every time I have those hard days, it's like I can feel the Enemy trying to kick me when I'm down and continue to push my buttons. I've always deeply struggled with impatience. Not necessarily impatience in relationships, just impatience for trivial and small things in my day going wrong. So when every *little* thing goes wrong in my day, it feels like one *big* mess.

Recently, I had the worst day I've had in a while where little things kept going wrong. I got up in the morning on my usual routine, got my three-month-old daughter up to feed her, and she woke up in a cranky and fussy mood. Tired from lack of sleep, I sluggishly walked down my stairs to make my coffee and noticed the water in our Keurig was low, so I had to fill it. When I went to put the filter back onto the coffee machine, I accidentally smacked it on the counter and water shot up and spilled all over me and the counter.

After cleaning up my mess, I walked into the living room and my sweet dog, Bernie, barfed all over our couch and continued to throw up the rest of the day. When I went to grab the pet cleaner to clean up his vomit, I stubbed my toe on the chair in my kitchen. Mind you, my baby was crying while all this was going on. Total chaos. So, of course, I picked her up to soothe her and she spit up all down my shirt and bra.

Girl, it just kept going and going. One thing after another, all day long. I had even gone upstairs in my bathroom at one point to try to wash my face in an attempt to wash away my bad attitude and noticed I was experiencing postpartum hair loss. That was it. I collapsed on the cold tile floor because I couldn't handle one more thing going wrong. Everything kept piling up. I had reached my breaking point. I felt utterly and completely defeated.

Remember how I told you that I have a problem with impatience? Imagine an adult temper tantrum. Are you imagining it? Arms thrown up, sobbing, sighing, throwing stuff, swearing, and so forth. That's exactly what happened afterward. I threw myself an epic pity party. I lost my ever-loving mind and exploded in a fit of rage because it felt like nothing was going right for me. I allowed my anger and my circumstances to get the best of me. I felt like a complete failure. In that moment I lost sight of who I was and whose I was.

In my frustration, I heard his gentle voice speak to my heart: *Do your circumstances have the power to change or dictate who you are and who I am?*

Wow. Talk about love covering over a multitude of sins. I knew I had sinned in my anger by cursing and having an ungrateful heart because of how my day was going. But in that moment, God's gentle love guided me back into who I really am.

On my rough day, I felt God ask me these four questions:

1. Is the goodness of God reliant on your circumstances?
2. Does your worth and value remain intact when everything is goes wrong?
3. What "buttons" in you are being pushed by the Enemy?
4. How are you going to shine the light of Christ in even the worst of circumstances?

Prompted by the Holy Spirit, I took a moment to ponder these questions. As I did so, I was able to invite God into my frustration. I acknowledged the difficulty I was facing in that moment, and I asked him to help me shift my heart and mind. It didn't change the fact that I had a hard day, but it did change my perspective. I decided to cancel my pity party, and I no longer believed a bad day equated a bad life.

When our circumstances fall apart, that's not the time for us to give up. That's the time for us to fall before God's feet and take our problems to his throne. But I'll be honest with you: everything I know about my identity gets pushed aside when I'm dealing with impatience and anger. Like when we go to church and worship the Lord, hear a compelling message, and enjoy fellowshipping with other brothers and sisters in Christ . . . then on the ride home someone cuts us off in traffic and we honk at them in anger.

This is where the rubber meets the road, friend. These are the moments we allow things to either make us or break us. The devil wants you to fix your eyes on your circumstances and not on who Jesus is in the midst of them.

Are we going to rise above our circumstances, challenged but unchanged by them and looking like Christ all the more? Or are we going to allow our circumstances to crush us and dictate whether or not we are okay?

This isn't talked about enough, which is why it needs to be exposed. The Enemy will try to use our circumstances to infiltrate our hearts. If our identity is tied to what's happening around us instead of Christ within us, this tactic will destroy us. He wants you to forget all that God has done and who he is so you'll focus on your unfortunate circumstances instead of the unwavering goodness of God in whom your true worth and identity are anchored. So the Enemy piles one wrong thing on top of another, hoping you'll buckle under the pressure of it all. And he doesn't limit his activity to little things like water spills and dog barf. Sometimes the Enemy pulls out the big guns and piles one life-devastating event on top of the other. In fact, that's exactly what he did with a man named Job.

The Lesson of Job

Job was known for being a good, upright man who loved God. "He was the greatest man among all the people of the East" (Job 1:3). He was considered righteous in the sight of God and man. Job was extremely wealthy: his livestock numbered in the thousands, he had ten children and numerous servants, and he was highly respected in his community. Satan accused Job before God, basically saying that if all the things in his life that were good suddenly took a turn for the worse, where his health, his family's lives, and everything around him essentially turned to dust and ruins, Job would no longer praise and worship God because all his blessings would be stripped away. Satan wanted to prove to God that Job's dedication was purely circumstantial and rooted in his prosperity. His accusation went something like this: "Job only praises you because you bless him. Take everything away, and he'll curse you to your face."

So, with God's permission, Satan afflicted Job in almost every area of his life. Of course Job was devastated, feeling all the emotions and turmoil of what was happening to him. But he remained stead-fast and faithful to God, praising him even in the hard. He refused to curse God or blame God because Job knew that even in the worst of circumstances, God's goodness doesn't change.

Can you imagine what Job must have gone through? Some scholars believe that the story of Job is an allegory that we can learn from and not an actual event that took place. Either way, Job lost literally everything, and yet he still chose to praise God. His affection for and dedication to God wasn't rooted in how blessed he was or how good he had it.

Now don't forget, Job felt the crushing weight of the devastation that his suffering had inflicted. The point is that he didn't allow his pain to be the indicator of God's goodness and his worship toward God.

We cannot allow our circumstance to dictate what we believe about our identity. Even when the sky is falling and our world is falling apart, who we are in Christ remains the same. We need to separate our experiences from what we know to be true about God. We need to remember who we are and whose we are despite what's happening around us. Job's story is a lesson for every believer under trial to focus on God rather than their circumstances. That's how we root ourselves in our relationship with God—secure in him no matter what comes our way.

We can't worship the gifts and blessings; we have to worship the one who gives them. And we can't define our relationship with God based on our prosperity and blessings. Not only is that bad theology, but it's also low-identity thinking. The rain falls on the righteous and the unjust (Matthew 5:45). So when trials come our way (notice we said *when*, not *if*) and those gifts and blessings fall away, we can stand firm in who we are because our identity isn't placed in how great things are going for us.

We can't afford to allow ourselves to live by feelings and emotions alone.

We can't afford to live our lives dictated by our circumstances.

We need to become rooted and established in Christ. Becoming more like him each day.

And that looks like facing the hardest circumstances and sinking our roots deeper as we stand firm in who we are in him and who he is.

God never promises us good, perfect, and happy days where everything goes right for us all the time. But he does promise that he will never leave or forsake us. Even in our suffering, we can still trust God and remain secure in him. God knows the pain we go through, and he is always with us. That's a promise we can rely on.

God has said,

> "Never will I leave you;
> never will I forsake you."

So we say with confidence,

> "The Lord is my helper; I will not be afraid.
> What can mere mortals do to me?"
> (Hebrews 13:5–6)

Life will most certainly deal us more than we can handle, but there's nothing God can't handle. He is our ever-present help in times of trouble (Psalm 46:1). When life becomes more than we can bear, God will always be there. His love will see us through. And remember: God *is* love. What would it look like if we spread a little of that love around, even as we face our times of trouble?

Becoming Love

It's time to stop partnering with low-identity thinking and start seeing ourselves and others as highly favored and precious in the eyes of our Father. If we are created in his image and he is love, then that's what we are to become. Friend, you are loved and precious in his sight.

It's not, "You are loved *if* you fix this and change that." No. You *are* loved by God, and that is it. You are precious in his sight in this moment. Right now. He loves you because love is literally what he is (1 John 4:8). Not only were you created in his image, but your life has great value to God. Scripture says we are co-laborers with God (1 Corinthians 3:9). And we have the incredible privilege of loving others by co-laboring with God (or co-loving).

Why would his Word say this if our lives didn't significantly matter to him? In Paul's first letter to the church at Corinth, he explained that each of us has a unique assignment as we co-labor in carrying out God's work.

What, after all, is Apollos? And what is Paul? Only servants, through whom you came to believe—as the Lord has assigned to each his task. I planted the seed, Apollos watered it, but God has been making it grow. So neither the one who plants nor the one who waters is anything, but only God, who makes things grow. The one who plants and the one who waters have one purpose, and they will each be rewarded according to their own labor. (1 Corinthians 3:5–8)

Note the distinction Paul made at the end—that we have different assignments but one purpose. That purpose is to enlarge the kingdom, which we do by loving well. This means you are essential to God's kingdom work. What you do, how you represent him—it all matters.

We get to wake up each day and be his children and shine the light and love of Christ everywhere we go. That purpose remains unchanged by whatever our circumstances may be. It simply requires being love in action to those around us.

Even if we are mistreated or rejected, we don't have to allow sin against us to produce sin within us. When we co-labor with God in loving others, we are called to love even those who are hard to love. "Love your enemies," Jesus said. "Do good to those who hate you" (Luke 6:27).

Although it's hard to imagine loving those who hurt us, it helps if we can start with compassion. We can try to see them through the lens of love by understanding they have wounds and struggles just like we do.

Choosing to love difficult people doesn't invalidate the pain you've suffered, nor does it require giving those who have harmed you access to you. But it does acknowledge the fact that those who have hurt us are likely carrying their own pain and are in need of the same mercy we have access to. To become love, we must first understand what the Bible says about love.

You've heard it before: "Love is patient, love is kind. It does not envy, it does not boast, it is not proud. It does not dishonor others, it is not self-seeking, it is not easily angered, it keeps no record of wrongs. Love does not delight in evil but rejoices with the truth. It always protects, always trusts, always hopes, always perseveres" (1 Corinthians 13:4–7).

I (Cass) find it fascinating that Paul made a point to tell us not only what love is but also what love isn't. Love isn't rude, slanderous, jealous, selfish, manipulative, or deceptive. Now that we understand what love is and isn't, let's talk about a few examples of how we can tangibly become the love this world desperately needs.

We become love when we seek justice and defend the oppressed. (Isaiah 1:17)

We become love when we see a need and meet a need. (Proverbs 3:27)

We become love when we offer hospitality. (1 Peter 4:9)

We become love when we advocate for the marginalized. (Proverbs 31:8–9)

We become love when we comfort those who mourn. (Matthew 5:4)

We become love when we carry each other's burdens. (Galatians 6:2)

We become love when we give generously. (Luke 6:38)

We become love when we are kind, compassionate, and forgiving. (Ephesians 4:32)

We become love when we share the gospel with the lost. (Mark 16:15)

We become love when we consider the needs of others. (Philippians 2:3–4)

In a world that is abundant with criticism and strife, it's important that we live our lives in a way that leads people to Christ. We have the incredible privilege of partnering with God by becoming vessels of his mercy for all the world to see. Becoming love is what we must do, and that starts with simply loving the person in front of you. But God doesn't just send us out completely unprotected, bleeding hearts on our sleeves. He gives holy armor to protect the ones he loves so we can lovingly reach others while defending against the Enemy of our souls.

Armor Up, Sister

When I (Britt) was in college, I was a part of a choir group. I was studying music education and needed to take a course in music performance. Since I love to sing, choir was the perfect fit. Unfortunately, at the time, I had so much going on in my life that my studies kind of fell behind.

I always sang soprano in choir in high school. If you don't know what that is, it's basically the highest voice, and it usually takes the melody in the choir. Well, when I began college, I ended up being put in the spot of an alto, which is basically a lower voice that structurally makes up the choir; altos usually sing the harmonies.

For example, when you hear a choir only sing melody, everybody is singing the exact same notes at the same time. But when you throw an alto or tenor in there to sing harmonies, that's what elevates the sound and makes it come alive. You can suddenly hear not just one sound but many sounds coming together and complementing one another beautifully.

Anyway, this was my first time as an alto in a choir setting. I quickly learned that it takes some serious understanding of where your notes are so the piece you are performing is perfect. You can't fake it until you make it when you're an alto. You've gotta know your notes and sing them with confidence. When I was in high school choir, my choir teacher was always getting on the altos to belt their notes out because of how important their lines were in making the harmonies loud and clear. Because everybody can hear the melody; it's the harmony that adds the dimension.

My college choir had a big, important concert coming up. Of course, being the procrastinator I was back then (and still am sometimes), I didn't practice my notes or practice any of the songs we were to perform—at all. When I say "at all," I mean I hadn't even glanced at my sheet music. Nineteen-year-old me was not very responsible when it came to taking my studies seriously. Oh, and by the way, the songs we were singing in this concert were in Latin, too, so that was really fun, considering I hadn't rehearsed my harmonies for each piece. I honestly thought I was going to be able to show up and just wing it.

Have you ever done that? Thought you could just skid by unprepared and everything would turn out perfectly? I'm sure that works sometimes, but it never really leaves you feeling like you did the best job you could. And girl, was it a bad idea for me to just wing it at my choir concert attempting to sing songs in Latin and nail my harmonies.

The day of the big choir concert arrived, and I was so nervous. I purposely didn't invite my mom, dad, or brothers because I knew it was going to be a disaster for me. I knew I wasn't going to be able to wing it. I felt like I'd arrived at school to take a really important exam that I hadn't studied for. Or like I'd stepped out on the pitcher's mound and didn't even know how to throw a ball. Anxiety kept building and building, and then it was time to line up in position.

As the lights beamed down on me and I stood there in my choir robe, I felt exposed—like everybody was going to know that I had no clue what I was doing. Nobody in the crowd likely noticed that I was clueless, but my choir director noticed right away. I had to literally lip sync to the songs and do my best to make it look like I knew what I was doing, even though I clearly didn't. And he knew I didn't know the pieces. He looked right at me during most of each song because he could very apparently tell that I was lost and hadn't rehearsed.

I look back now and laugh at this story, but I remember how embarrassed I felt. All my embarrassment could've been easily avoided had I just taken the time to prepare. I had the sheet music, and I was provided with everything I needed to prepare, but I dropped the ball and didn't place any importance on it. Honestly, why did I even show up to the concert if I didn't know what I was doing? I probably embarrassed my choir director too.

Isn't it good news that we don't have to feel unprepared for spiritual battle?

Friend, this isn't easy. You're going to have to combat the daily temptation of believing that anything outside of God has the power to define you. The Enemy does not want this truth to stick, and he does not want you to stand firm. He does not want you to be a force for God's love in the world.

One of my absolute favorite Bible passages about combating the deception of the Enemy comes from Paul's letter to the church at Ephesus.

> Be strong in the Lord and in his mighty power. Put on the full armor of God, so that you can take your stand against the devil's schemes. For our struggle is not against flesh and blood, but against the rulers, against the authorities, against the powers of this dark world and against the spiritual forces of evil in the heavenly realms. Therefore put on the full armor of God, so that when the day of evil comes, you may be able to stand your ground, and after you have done everything, to stand. (Ephesians 6:10–13)

God gives us the armor we need to protect ourselves in spiritual battles and detailed instructions on how to combat the deception of the Enemy. When the Enemy catches us off guard, he has a strategic advantage. I thank God every day for the preparation he gives us to endure trials because it's never fun to feel unprepared for something.

This is why God so graciously gave us the most beautiful instruction manual on how to extinguish the Enemy's flaming arrows: the Bible. We don't have to fake it till we make it because he has given us clear instructions in his Word on how to handle spiritual warfare.

Like we have mentioned previously, our spiritual enemy, the devil, is actively seeking to kill, steal, and destroy. He hates God and all believers. We don't have to step out onto the battlefield unprepared without anything to protect us or use as a weapon. It may seem strenuous to have to suit up in the armor of God every day, but with prayer and practice, we can better understand and implement habits of putting on our armor each day.

Let's armor up, sister, and look at the resources God gives us as listed in Ephesians 6:13–18:

- *Sword of the Spirit:* The Word of God. His Word is our defensive and offensive weapon. This means we can use it to protect us and to also drive out danger. It cuts through bones and flesh and is sharper than any double-edged sword.
- *Belt of Truth:* Truth keeps us from falling for deception.
- *Shield of Faith:* Faith in God protects us when we are tempted with doubt.
- *Breastplate of Righteousness:* In Christ we are right with God, and he will guard our hearts.

- *Helmet of Salvation:* Our salvation comes from Jesus. The battlefield in our minds is the primary place spiritual battle is fought. Protect your mind by resting in the finished work of the cross and your salvation in Christ.
- *Feet prepared with the gospel of peace:* The gospel of peace keeps our feet anchored and standing firm.

It's only when we put on the full armor of God that we are truly prepared for battle. The weapons of the Enemy might form against us, but they will not prosper (Isaiah 54:17). Let's take back the Enemy territory one day at a time through prayer and living the Word. Your actions matter. Your prayers matter. They make a difference in this world.

Tried, Purified, and Trustworthy

There's something inspiring about being around someone who has fought hard battles and yet continues to walk in victory. It makes you dare to believe that you can be free too.

Each fire we walk through is just another way that Christ refines us. To be around someone who is undoubtedly free, despite the difficulty they've experienced, gives us a sense of comfort that we, too, can overcome adversity and rise above our circumstances despite the trials we're currently facing. The Bible has a lot to say about refinement. The process of purification requires the furnace of affliction.

The psalmist wrote:

You, O God, have tested us;

    you have tried us as silver is tried.

You brought us into the net;

    you laid a crushing burden on our backs;

you let men ride over our heads;

    we went through fire and through water;

yet you have brought us out to a place of

    abundance.

(Psalm 66:10–12 ESV)

Again, we tend to trust the experiences of those who have walked through the refining fires of life. Their sooty faces tell us the story of their resilience and reliance on God. The singed fabric of their clothing reminds us that they've pressed on and endured through the trying of their faith. It's difficult to lean on the experiences of those who have never walked through something similar to what you're facing. That's why it's important for us as believers to tell the stories of what we've walked through; it equips others and emboldens them to believe they can persevere through Jesus too.

Contagious Freedom

Over the years of my personal walk with Jesus, I (Cass) have learned that freedom is contagious—and it loves company!

I remember when I first truly submitted my life to God. I was nineteen years old, and I had started attending a popular college church filled with loud music, bright lights, and friendly faces. This was the type of place where you could leave your baggage at the door. Upon entry you sensed the freedom in the atmosphere mixed with the thick aroma of AXE body spray. This church was unlike anything I had ever encountered before. If Christianity had a club scene, this place would have been it. From the moment I walked in the door, worship music was on full blast, and I could sense that I belonged without knowing a single soul. There was an intensity about the people I encountered there that threw me off at first. Their zeal for the Lord was slightly disorienting, and it took time for me to get acclimated.

I wasn't used to being surrounded by so much light! The joy and vibrancy these people gave off was almost blinding for someone like me. I wasn't sure what it was about these church people that was different, but they were definitely different. Whatever it was, I was both intimidated and intrigued by it. I wanted whatever it was that they had. I wanted to know what they knew. I wanted Jesus to infiltrate my life like that too.

During my time attending this church, I watched drug dealers break the bondage of addiction and become respected leaders within the ministry. I watched people throw pills in the trash and pour entire bottles of vodka down the ladies' bathroom sink. I watched people pitch in to buy groceries for a friend in need. I watched young women with unplanned pregnancies be showered with genuine affection and support.

It was the first time I had ever encountered the tangible, transformative power of Jesus up close, and it became personal. I saw the freedom the people around me encountered, and it changed me. I watched people who were once defined by their circumstances and dead in their sin become something totally new. I craved the same freedom for myself.

There's a reason Scripture says that we overcome our accuser by the blood of the Lamb and the word of our testimonies (Revelation 12:11). You can't argue with a changed life!

A few years into the infancy of my walk with Jesus, I became deeply affected by the influence of an acquaintance. We'll call her Spiritual Sally. I never actually became close friends with Sally, but I admired her walk with the Lord from a distance.

To this day, she's still one of the most beautiful people I've ever seen in real life. Sally had endured difficult trials throughout her life, but the way she had allowed those experiences to inform her walk with God inspired me. She was fearless in the way she went about sharing her faith, and when she worshipped it was like no one else was in the room. Her tenacity through trials reminded me that our circumstances don't get the final say.

I remember being at a church service on a Thursday night when I noticed Sally walking around the room silently praying. She was pacing back and forth. My eyes followed her around the room. I have no idea what was on her mind, and honestly I probably should've been minding my own business, but I happened to look up, and there she was in full-on prayer mode, marching around the sanctuary like she was dismantling the Enemy and petitioning God all at once. Watching her freely express herself and her trust in God gave me freedom to do the same.

The way she lived uninhibited by the opinions of others pushed me to be brave, and as I continued to mature in my faith,

I slowly became able to do the same. There came a point in my life when I caught myself wondering, *What would Spiritual Sally do?*

At that moment I realized I was modeling my life after the overflow of someone else's walk with Jesus instead of leaning on Jesus alone. Don't get me wrong; having godly influences in our lives is a good thing. As a matter of fact, it's essential. But we must never lose sight of Jesus.

Despite all the hard things Sally walked through, her relationship with Jesus deeply affected my own. My love for God deepened, and my trust in Jesus was strengthened. That's what I mean when I say freedom is contagious.

Friend, there's a reason your testimony is so important. Because your life lived is better than any sermon you could ever preach. The world is watching and waiting for us to practice the words we preach. It's desperately looking for tangible evidence of the love of God we say dwells within us.

Your life creates a ripple effect far beyond your immediate circle. Your faith in Jesus, lived out, leads others to wonder what this Christianity thing is all about. We have the privilege of being a part of God's divine mission to save the world! The freedom we have access to will ignite hope in the hearts of those around us if we're willing to share it.

Freedom loves company, friend. Show up as you are, where you're at, with what you've got, and watch God use it all. God can use you right now no matter what you've been through or what you've done. Your trials and circumstances don't wield the power to define you. God within you and through you is all that truly matters.

When we decide to live our lives firmly established in our worth in Christ instead of living to obtain worth, we offer others permission to do the same. Let's go live our lives in a way that leads others to the hope we have in him. Let's live loved and become the love this world desperately needs.

Ready, set, *go!*

Reflect and Respond

1. Is it hard for you to believe in the goodness of God on hard days? Why or why not?

2. Have you ever allowed your circumstances to cause you to lose sight of who you are and whose you are? If so, how will you combat this train of thought in the future?

3. What was your immediate reaction to reading that you are loved and precious to God? How has this truth affected your life?

4. Have you experienced contagious freedom in your life? What did it look like?

5. Do you have a Spiritual Sally in your life? Can you think of someone whose tenacity through trials inspires your walk with God and encourages your own?

Ten

Course Correcting

It's Not Too Late to Turn Down the Right Path

HAVE YOU EVER GOTTEN LOST on a road trip? Have you typed the address into Google Maps and then realized that you missed your exit after going miles in the wrong direction? I (Britt) have done this!

I specifically remember driving to Indiana to visit my husband, who was my boyfriend at the time. As I was driving and listening to music, I looked over and saw my husband's best friend, Dustin, in his car, waving and laughing at me on the road.

Confused, I waved back with a nervous little giggle because I knew he was traveling *to* Michigan from Indiana that day to visit his girlfriend, and I was traveling *from* Michigan to Indiana to visit my boyfriend. Why was he going in the same direction as me? Clearly one of us had to be going in the wrong direction! Next thing I knew, I got a call from my boyfriend. With laughter in his voice, he asked me why I was driving east on I-94 when I was supposed to be going west. *Um, that's a good question!* I was annoyed because I thought I had been following where the GPS was taking me the entire time. It must have happened when I stopped at a gas station to fill up and resumed my trip. When I jumped back on the highway, apparently, I made a small but huge mistake. Right highway, wrong direction. I went about thirty miles out of my way without even realizing it!

There I was having a good old time listening to my music and going in the wrong direction for more than thirty minutes! I've actually done things like this before, but this time I thought it was hilarious to randomly see my boyfriend's best friend waving at me. I'm also relieved I saw him—because I could have driven all the way back home without realizing it. How frustrating to waste a big chunk of time and a lot of gasoline going in the wrong direction! I quickly got off at an exit and proceeded in the right direction.

My husband reminds me of this event from time to time when we travel. But I tend to think about it whenever I need to make a course correction in life.

U-Turns in the Right Direction

Just like my (Britt's) directional mishap, we can end up going the wrong direction in our lives, sometimes without fully realizing it. It can happen when we don't have a firm foundation or a fertile soil like what we talked about in chapter 8. Sin can pull us in the wrong direction and away from God. Sometimes we know we are traveling in the wrong direction, but the pain and discomfort of turning away from our sin is too heavy to bear, so we continue without realizing we are creating more pain for ourselves in the long run.

The important part of my highway story was that when I noticed I was on the wrong path, I got off the highway and turned onto the right path. I didn't continue to go down the wrong road. I changed course. I did a U-turn and proceeded in the right direction.

If you are traveling and notice you're going the wrong way, it'd be kind of silly to know that but continue to head in the wrong direction, right? Why, then, do we do this in our lives when we're headed in the wrong direction and away from God? Maybe the road away from him feels temporarily satisfying, but I can assure you it always leads to destruction.

Jesus put it this way: "Enter through the narrow gate. For wide is the gate and *broad is the road that leads to destruction*, and many enter through it. But small is the gate and narrow the road that leads to life, and only a few find it" (Matthew 7:13–14, emphasis added).

Unfortunately, sometimes the road that leads to destruction is the most appealing. It's the most comfortable route that everybody else takes. It's really wide and spacious, full of other cars, and doesn't look so lonely. It probably has the nicest pavement with the fanciest rest stops. But all the fancy bells and whistles fall void in comparison to traveling down the road that leads to everlasting life. The road less traveled. The road that challenges you. I can assure you—this is the road you *want* to be on. The narrow road is the only road that leads to eternal life. There is only *one* way that leads to Jesus. He said, "I am the way and the truth and the life. No one comes to the Father except through me" (John 14:6).

We are here on this earth for such a small amount of time. It's a single grain of sand on the beaches of eternity. Why waste time going in the wrong direction when you can merge onto the narrow road that leads to eternity with God?

It's said that the road to hell is paved with good intentions. Although it sounds harsh, it's true. Often we find ourselves traveling toward destruction one compromise at a time. A warning sign that you need to make a U-turn is not there if the fruit of the Spirit is no longer evident in your life (Galatians 5:22–23). When we begin to lack love, joy, peace, patience, kindness, goodness, faithfulness, gentleness, and self-control, it's likely we're veering off course.

If you have been traveling down the wrong road, it's not too late to turn down the right one, friend. It's not too late to change course. I don't care if you've gone hours or even years in the wrong direction; if you have a pulse, *it's not too late.* Much like my story of traveling in the wrong direction, it would be wasteful to continue onto the wrong path.

How do we know where the narrow road is? The good news is that the Lord says:

I will instruct you and teach you in the way you
    should go;
I will counsel you with my loving eye on you.
Do not be like the horse or the mule,
    which have no understanding
but must be controlled by bit and bridle
    or they will not come to you.
Many are the woes of the wicked,
    but the LORD's unfailing love
    surrounds the one who trusts in him.
(Psalm 32:8–10)

How beautiful that he tenderly looks after us and teaches us in the way we should go. He lovingly shows us the path we should be on, and anytime temptation tries to make us veer off course, he always provides the detour to get right back onto the narrow road.

No temptation has overtaken you except what is common to mankind. And God is faithful; he will not let you be tempted beyond what you can bear. But when you are tempted, he will also provide a way out so that you can endure it. (1 Corinthians 10:13)

So, when we feel tempted or we become distracted by whatever the Enemy is dangling in front of us, let's tune into the Lord's voice and follow him back in the right direction. The scripture above reminds us that the Lord will always provide a way out, so let's take it.

At one point in my life, I was going in the wrong direction even after I was saved. It broke my heart once I realized where I was heading, and the Lord convicted me that I was living in sin. But I kept going and not repenting or departing from my sin. I knew I was going in the wrong direction and just kept traveling until I realized I was headed toward destruction.

I got saved when I was nineteen years old, and I was so on fire for Jesus. I was like a little baby in the Lord, just in awe and wonder of who he is. The Word says to receive Christ like a child (Mark 10:15), but I hadn't known how to apply his Word to my life just yet. The fire in me burned out because I allowed myself to fall back into temptation and sin. I was surrounded by the wrong people and not mature enough as a Christian to withstand temptation in the presence of other people who were living in sin.

I was in an on-again, off-again relationship with someone at the time who was not a Christian. I found the Lord while I was in that relationship because I was in such a state of despair. In that relationship, I was committing all sorts of sin with that person. I felt trapped in a toxic cycle and didn't know how to get out of it.

I remember one day specifically when I kept pleading with the Lord to cleanse me of all unrighteousness and to give me the strength to walk away from this relationship. I knew it was keeping me from really pursuing God with everything I had in me. He answered my prayer on a day I needed it the most. I was able to walk away from the toxic mess I was in and repent of my sin. I turned onto the right road and continued with God.

I think we all veer off course from time to time. The important part is that once you see you are going in the wrong direction, you can quickly turn around, repent, and change course. Just like me, there will be times that you might fall off the path for a moment. But you can get right back onto the route he has laid out for you.

God's Word says, "I am convinced that neither death nor life, neither angels nor demons, neither the present nor the future, nor any powers, neither height nor depth, nor anything else in all creation, will be able to separate us from the love of God that is in Christ Jesus our Lord" (Romans 8:38–39).

The Enemy will try to tell you that you've gone too far so you might as well keep going where you are already headed. But Jesus is calling you to turn away and come to him. If this is you today, do the U-turn, friend. It's not too late, and the Lord's arms are wide open to you.

Next, we will look at how the Lord views us compared to how the Enemy views us. Understanding the difference can help you course correct even faster.

Jesus Calls You by Name

I (Britt) have always had a strength for remembering faces, but I struggle to remember names. I can recognize someone I saw one time in passing, but the moment you ask me what that person's name is, my mind draws a blank. My mom is the exact same way. So much that she will forget someone's name and then take a shot in the dark at what she thinks their name is, call them by that, and be totally wrong. It makes me laugh every time I witness her do this! Except for the time she forgot someone's name at a funeral. I felt embarrassed for her, but I've *definitely* been there.

As for Satan, he knows our names, but he would rather degrade us by calling us by our sins and weaknesses. He does this so we will take on those labels and identify with them.

- "You've got anger issues, and nobody will ever feel peace around you."
- "You're a person who says one thing and does another."
- "You're unreliable."
- "You're a liar."
- "You're a glutton and can't control yourself around food."
- "All you do is gossip; you'll never get it right."

The list goes on and on because Satan is the accuser. He will always label you by your sin to get you to think less of yourself. He sees you off track, and he wants to keep you there. He doesn't want you to identify as what God says you are in Christ and course correct. He also wants you to continue to relive and rehash your past to keep you in a state of captivity.

This tactic the Enemy uses is effective because it gets our focus on our sin and not on our Savior. And if our focus is not on our Savior, then we won't be compelled to turn away from our sin.

When the Enemy reminds you of your past, remember this verse: "If we confess our sins, he is faithful and just and will forgive us our sins and purify us from all unrighteousness" (1 John 1:9). Forgive and purify. That's a promise, and you can bank on it. We can trust God; he is faithful, and he will fulfill his promise. So if the Enemy tries to remind you, respond with "Forgiven and purified. Bye!"

Jesus, on the other hand, calls us by our names, not by our sins. He knows our sins; he knows where our hearts are. But he chooses to call us by our names instead. He chooses to see us for our created value instead of where we've fallen short.

There's something about hearing your name that grabs your attention. It heightens your awareness and causes your ear to turn toward whoever is calling you. When someone calls your name, your immediate thought might be, *Oh, that person knows who I am?!*

Now imagine Jesus saying your name. I don't know about you, but I get a feeling of security and comfort knowing that he knows me, sees me, and cares to speak to me. There is something about being known—truly known and truly loved. This makes me want to be back on the road pursuing Jesus. I want to run toward that kind of love.

The Enemy says: "You're off track. Might as well drive into a ditch and stay there."

The Lord says: "You're off track, dear one. I see you, and I'll love you back to me."

Friend, Jesus calls you by name because *he loves you, he chose you, he wants you, and he accepts you.* He doesn't call you by your sin because he is love, and his love for you covers over a multitude of sins (1 Peter 4:8).

> Do not fear, for I have redeemed you;
> > I have summoned you by name; you are mine.
> When you pass through the waters,
> > I will be with you;
> and when you pass through the rivers,
> > they will not sweep over you.
> When you walk through the fire,
> > you will not be burned;
> > the flames will not set you ablaze.
>
> (Isaiah 43:1–2)

God's Voice and Satan's Voice

Have you ever whispered a secret to anyone? You'll notice you have to get really close to that person to whisper what you want to say in their ear. You can't whisper to someone who is physically far away from you. You must draw near and be close so they can hear your words.

You see, when God speaks to us and calls our names, he always uses a still, small voice that is ever so close to us. Almost like a gentle whisper. I (Britt) find it so tenderly beautiful that he chooses to speak to us in this manner because it proves to us just how close he really is. *He is closer than our very breath.*

In contrast, the Enemy shouts at us because he is far. He shouts accusations left and right. He wants his voice to be the loudest because he's trying hard to dominate the gentle voice of God. I'm sure you've heard the popular saying, "The loudest voice in the room isn't always the right one." How true is that when it comes to God's voice versus Satan's voice?!

The loudest voice is always trying hard to be heard. The Enemy hopes you will listen and agree with him rather than with God. Going back to the driving analogy, it's like having Apple Maps and Google Maps open at the same time, and they are both competing to give you directions. I have noticed at times when I press into God's presence, the Enemy's voice tries to get louder. But the more I draw near to God and pursue him with my whole heart, the more the Enemy's voice gets drowned out.

So when you hear the Enemy shouting accusations at you, know that he is desperately trying to speak over the Word of God. Since the Enemy is the father of lies, let this be a reminder to you that what he is accusing you of, God is saying the exact opposite. The Enemy wants to silence God's voice in your life. We must know the difference between God's voice and the Enemy's voice.

Here's a practical way to decipher between God's voice and Satan's voice.

God's Voice

- calms
- comforts
- convicts
- encourages
- clarifies
- leads
- reassures
- is patient
- is gentle
- is kind
- strengthens
- heals
- gives
- instills hope
- forgives
- induces peace

Satan's Voice

- obsesses
- worries
- condemns
- discourages
- confuses
- brings about shame
- pushes
- frightens
- rushes
- weakens
- hurts
- steals
- causes despair
- accuses
- induces stress
- is cruel
- is harsh

As you can see, there is a very stark difference between the two. One is pure truth; one is deceitful lies. When it comes to what you believe about yourself, you must decide who you will listen to. Who do you agree with? Let's make it even simpler. Do you want to align your thoughts with the biggest liar of all time? Of course not. Let's remember him for who he is: the liar of all liars.

I'll leave you with this:

God says you are blessed.
The Enemy says you are cursed.
You get to cast the final vote.
You are the tiebreaker.

The Way That Seems Right

At one point in my life, I (Britt) was in such a deep state of depression that I didn't even want to leave my house. It was when I first got married. I had moved from Michigan to Indiana to be with my husband and left all my family and friends. I guess I didn't realize how much that would affect me because I always thought I was someone who could adapt to change pretty easily. Everything was fine at first, and I was blissfully unaware of how homesick I actually was. Of course, I was happy with my husband, and our marriage was beautiful. I just had so much pain stored away in my heart, and I wasn't taking any of my pain to Jesus. I was afraid of this new life being a wife.

What if I fail?
What if I'm a bad wife?
What if my husband gets sick of me now that we live together?

Fear will do that to ya.

I was also battling a binge eating disorder, and I had gained a lot of weight from it. I felt alone and didn't know anybody in Indiana other than my husband. I missed my family and felt forgotten about and left out once I moved away. I think I just froze and felt afraid to pursue any kind of new friendships because my weight gain held me back from wanting to be around anybody, especially anybody new. So I'd hide. I'd stay inside all day. My husband's job made more than enough money to support us, so I was a stay-at-home wife for a period of time. (There's absolutely nothing wrong with that. I just literally didn't do anything all day and sat in laziness.)

I'd sit in my living room in the dark and watch Netflix and eat Doritos. Cool Ranch Doritos, to be specific. I couldn't muster the courage to get myself up and motivated to start the day, so I'd waste away on the couch all day long with Dorito dust on my lap. How sad it was to see myself sitting in despair and inaction like that. Yet, I would stay paralyzed from taking any action because remaining stagnant was easier than confronting what was actually causing me pain. I was comfortable not doing anything at all. Lots of shows; lots of Doritos. Isn't it funny that we will continue to writhe in pain far too long before going to the Healer?

One time I decided to walk outside for a moment to get some fresh air because I felt like I really needed it. When I opened the door and let the light shine on me, it almost hurt because I was so accustomed to sitting in the dark. It made me want to be in the light more. You know how when you walk outside, the light almost blinds you because you haven't seen it in a while? My eyes immediately squinted shut as I scrunched my face while standing in the sun. I felt like a vampire. But the sun beating down on my skin made me feel warm yet exposed at the same time.

Geez, how long has it been since I've been out in the sun? I asked myself this right away when I realized the drastic difference of being outside and what it did for my soul.

Much like stepping out into the sun from the darkness, when I met with God in my state of despair, it was like drinking water in a dry, barren land. I hadn't realized how far away from him I had wandered until I did an about-face to go back home to him.

Sure, I could've stayed paralyzed on my couch for many more years, never confronting my pain or the sin I was living in—gluttony, laziness, watching lustful shows and movies, and so forth. It was satisfying to do nothing and hide inside all day. I felt comfortable in my own little bubble. But I was never going to find healing when I was self-inflicting more wounds and literally and figuratively sitting in darkness.

Jesus is always better than the temporary fix.

The temporary fix will do just that, temporarily mask the issue so you don't have to feel the pain from it. You might feel better, but it's not actually better *for* you. It will never lead you to permanent peace and ultimate healing unless it's brought to Jesus. The wisdom of Scripture says, "There is a way which seems right to a person, but its end is the way of death" (Proverbs 14:12 NASB). We must course correct.

If the "fix" feels good to your flesh, chances are it likely isn't good for your spirit. Here are some common fixes:

- sex
- loving money
- giving in to lust
- idolatry
- gluttony
- gossip
- slandering or tearing down others
- envy
- addiction

The good news is that with Jesus we don't need the Band-Aid of temporary fixes. He is our ultimate Healer, and he is our Redeemer.

Whatever temporary fixes you might be using today, repent, put them aside, and approach his throne. Open your hands and receive his permanent peace, and let the power of his presence be what gives you the strength to overcome the pain.

Silencing Shame, Embracing Grace

Guilt, condemnation, and shame—these are three tools Satan uses to keep us from making U-turns when we're headed down the wrong road.

Guilt: "I'm not forgiven."
Condemnation: "I deserve judgment."
Shame: "It's still who I am."

None of this is the gospel. These three tools cause us to run from God and hide from him instead of running to him.

Shame is one of the heaviest, most humiliating burdens a person can carry. It can make situations linger in your head and replay repeatedly. Shame will also try to identify you as the mistake you've made.

Just thinking about the things that have caused shame for us can make us want to go and hide in the corner with our eyes covered. Unfortunately, shame will hijack our peace and tag along for the ride when we try to bury it instead of bringing it to the cross.

Shame has afflicted us since the garden when Adam and Eve bit into the fruit God told them not to eat and they suddenly realized they were naked. Their first instinct was to hide because they knew what they had done was wrong (Genesis 3). They hid from each other and from God.

We live with this same instinct to hide ourselves when we are living in sin. Here are some examples of how the voices of guilt, shame, and condemnation speak into our lives:

Guilt: "I've messed up *too* much. I've gone *too* far."

Shame: "I'm going to hide from God and remain in darkness because I'll never change or get it right. This is who I am now—*my mistakes.*"

Condemnation: "God is going to be so mad at me. There's *no way* he can love me or forgive me after what I've done."

You see how the Enemy works in this?

Guilt makes you feel shame, then shame becomes your identity and speaks condemnation over you. Because the lie is, *How could you ever possibly be forgiven for what you've done? You are too dirty. You are too broken.*

Remember: the Enemy doesn't want God's grace, love, and mercy for your life. If he can get you in a place of guilt, condemnation, or shame, then he can keep you hidden away in darkness and from God, believing lies and never entering into the truth.

But take heart, friend:

In Christ Jesus, you are not condemned.

You are not broken.

You are not dirty.

You are not guilty.

Shame does not have to rule over you any longer.

You are not a mistake.

You are not your mistake.

You've just made mistakes.

God's love is greater than any shame that has found you.

Only he can address the life-threatening weight of shame.

May the covering of God's love silence the shame in
your life.

May you find freedom in the mercy and grace that is found
only in Jesus.

Scripture says that "there is now no condemnation for those who are in Christ Jesus" (Romans 8:1). Praise God for that! God wants a heart turned toward him in godly sorrow, not condemnation. Paul said to the Corinthians:

> Yet now I am happy, not because you were made sorry, but because your sorrow led you to repentance. For you became sorrowful as God intended and so were not harmed in any way by us. Godly sorrow brings repentance that leads to salvation and leaves no regret, but worldly sorrow brings death. (2 Corinthians 7:9–10)

Notice that this verse doesn't say that shame led to repentance, but godly sorrow does.

It's God's goodness and kindness that lead us to repentance, not shame (Romans 2:4). Godly sorrow convicts us to change, whereas shame causes us to hide from God and to stay hidden. When we trust Jesus as our righteousness and our provider of everything we need, shame will lose its power over us.

That's what happened to the Samaritan woman at the well in John chapter 4. This woman's life was an absolute wreck. After several marriages that failed, she no longer cared about the covenant of marriage and kept giving her body to men who weren't her husband. She had gone to the well so she could draw water alone and away from the condemning looks she was receiving from the other Samaritans. She was the outcast in town. When Jesus approached her and told her what he knew about her situation, she listened to Jesus and believed in him. Her sin-wrecked life was redeemed, and her shame was destroyed. She no longer had to hide. She was seen by Jesus for who she was instead of what she did.

Jesus didn't condemn the Samaritan woman or scold her; he loved her and was kind to her, believing better about her and seeing her for who she was created to be. Jesus can clothe us in a new wardrobe: *righteousness* instead of *shame*.

The promise of John 3:16 is *not* "God was so frustrated and exasperated that he sent his Son." No. The promise is "God so loved the world that he gave his one and only Son." God didn't send his Son because he was sick of us; he sent his Son to restore what had been lost. To eliminate the power of shame and guilt over our lives and stamp it with righteousness through Christ.

What does that look like? It looks like on your worst day grace is abounding even greater. On your darkest, most willful adventure, his love is pursuing you and saying, *Daughter, you are so much more than this, and I've known you from the beginning. I'm not changing my mind about you because my love for you never fails.*

Instead of listening to the voices of guilt, condemnation, and shame, you can allow grace, mercy, and love to speak into your life.

> *Grace:* "I acknowledge that I've sinned, and I'm going to boldly come before his throne of grace."
> *Mercy:* "I'm forgiven and brand new. I no longer have to be a slave to sin."
> *Love:* "I'm loved, accepted, and clean."

We can come to God's throne of grace with great confidence (Hebrews 4:16), for mercy and grace are in great abundance. We are saved by grace through faith. Grace and faith go hand in hand. The book of Hebrews tells us, "Without faith it is impossible to please God, because anyone who comes to him must believe that he exists and that he rewards those who earnestly seek him" (11:6). It's impossible to please God without what? *Faith.*

So when we are walking in faith, we are walking in the outpouring of his grace over our lives. Of course, we have to have godly sorrow for our sins, and there is a place for repentance, but we cannot preach his grace apart from his healing transformation. Grace doesn't allow us to live in the flesh; grace changes us. The grace of God is God's power. It's his ability to make us what we could never be on our own. Grace transforms us.

Walking in his grace is not the same as walking in awareness of sin. Yes, we have sinned, and we have fallen short of the glory of God (Romans 3:23). But it doesn't stop there. We aren't *just* sinners in need of a Savior but sinners who have been made new and redeemed into righteousness. We are created in Christ Jesus to do good works (Ephesians 2:10). We are no longer slaves of sin but slaves of righteousness through obedience to Jesus Christ (Romans 6:15–18).

It's not about living life every day and desperately trying *not* to sin. It's about walking in relationship with the Father and knowing in the deepest part of your soul that you are his daughter. Deeply loved. Cared for. Forgiven. Washed clean.

If we have the mindset of "trying not to sin," we are taking on the identity of a sinner, constantly afraid to trip up and mess

up. But what if we allow the gospel to shift our perspective of ourselves from "sinner" to "daughter"?

> Trying not to sin is the wrong focus.
> Being his beloved daughter is the right focus.

That's not to say you won't fall into sin at times, because you probably will. Just don't let yourself get stuck there and let the Enemy lie to you and tell you it's who you are and that you'll never change. You have been perfected in righteousness in Christ. So instead of waking up every day trying not to sin, wake up every day and be his daughter.

We have to consider ourselves dead to sin but alive to God. The apostle Paul put it this way:

> What shall we say, then? Shall we go on sinning so that grace may increase? By no means! We are those who have died to sin; how can we live in it any longer? Or don't you know that all of us who were baptized into Christ Jesus were baptized into his death? We were therefore buried with him through baptism into death in order that, just as Christ was raised from the dead through the glory of the Father, we too may live a new life.
>
> For if we have been united with him in a death like his, we will certainly also be united with him in a resurrection like his. For we know that our old self was crucified with him so that the body ruled by sin might be done away with, that we should no longer be slaves to sin—because anyone who has died has been set free from sin.

Now if we died with Christ, we believe that we will also live with him. For we know that since Christ was raised from the dead, he cannot die again; death no longer has mastery over him. The death he died, he died to sin once for all; but the life he lives, he lives to God. (Romans 6:1–10)

Being alive in Christ means taking on the new identity and mind of Christ. It means being stripped of sin and clothed in righteousness. He removes our shame and covers us with grace.

From dirty to clean.
From old to new.
From lost to found.

Remember:

Condemnation is a tool of the Enemy.
Conviction is a gift from the Holy Spirit.

One will shackle you to your worst moments; the other says, "Go and sin no more" (John 8:11 NLT).

Course-Correction Master

In the gospel of John, Jesus helped a woman caught in adultery make a major course correction. The teachers of the law were attempting to trap Jesus and use this woman as bait.

Jesus went to the Mount of Olives.

At dawn he appeared again in the temple courts, where all the people gathered around him, and he sat down to teach them. The teachers of the law and the Pharisees brought in a woman caught in adultery. They made her stand before the group and said to Jesus, "Teacher, this woman was caught in the act of adultery. In the Law Moses commanded us to stone such women. Now what do you say?" They were using this question as a trap, in order to have a basis for accusing him.

But Jesus bent down and started to write on the ground with his finger. When they kept on questioning him, he straightened up and said to them, "Let any one of you who is without sin be the first to throw a stone at her." Again he stooped down and wrote on the ground.

At this, those who heard began to go away one at a time, the older ones first, until only Jesus was left, with the woman still standing there. Jesus straightened up and asked her, "Woman, where are they? Has no one condemned you?"

"No one, sir," she said.

"Then neither do I condemn you," Jesus declared. "Go now and leave your life of sin." (John 8:1–11)

I (Cass) often wonder, *What was Jesus scribbling in the sand?* Some believe that he was writing down the sins of the men who hurled accusations at this woman. Maybe they, too, had "known" her. Maybe not. The mystery of what Jesus was writing is both alluring and intentional. We, the readers, can speculate about what was written in the dirt.

One thing is for certain: the men who were once convinced of their own righteousness walked away painfully aware of their own filth. Jesus wasn't messing around with the "Do as I say, not as I do" hypocrisy of these "religious" men.

How often are we the accusers, pointing our fingers at the sins of others? Seeing the worst in others while believing the best of ourselves. Woe to us, who lack the ability to see our own desperate need for repentance. If we were with Jesus that day, I wonder what would've been written in the gravel.

We know one thing for sure: our best is filthy rags, but Jesus gives us what we don't deserve—unmerited favor, tender mercy, and unconditional love. He strips us of shame and clothes us in righteousness through his grace and mercy.

In the chapter to come, we will be reminding ourselves of God's truth, especially when we need it.

Reflect and Respond

1. In what areas of your life do you need a course correction?
2. What are some of the lies the Enemy tries to get *you* to believe?
3. Is there any shame you are still carrying that you need to lay at the feet of Jesus?

4. Let's practice telling the difference between hearing the voice of God and Satan's voice. Fill in the blank in the following sentences:

I know that God is speaking when _____.

The voice of Satan sounds like _____.

Eleven

Remind Me Again
When We Forget Our Worth

WE ARE FORGETFUL. HECK, HALF the time we can't even remember what we had for breakfast this morning. And if both Cass and I (Britt) are being honest, we don't always remember our worth to God or who we are in him. Yes, sometimes we veer off course and get distracted. But we're thankful to have his Word to guide us right back. And you do, too, friend.

Because we are forgetful, it's critical to speak his truth over ourselves and apply his Word to our lives daily. Sister, we don't want to become like the man described by the apostle James who looked in the mirror but forgot what he looked like as soon as he walked away because he didn't do what the Word says (James 1:23–24).

You see, most people look in the mirror for a purpose—to

comb their hair, brush their teeth, or make sure they don't have toilet paper on their shoes—not just to stare mindlessly at their own reflections. Likewise, a healthy Christian reads the Bible not just to store up facts and knowledge that they'll never put to good use but to take action. We have to be hearers *and* doers, putting his Word into action every single day.

When we apply God's Word in our lives it becomes heart knowledge, not just words written on a page. In applying it, we're reminded of our true worth, secure in our identity, and confident in who we are in Christ. In the face of the Enemy's lies, we can keep our perspective clear. Even in the midst of adversity. Taking action also helps us stay rooted and grounded, established in the truth of God's love for us as demonstrated by Christ's sacrifice.

While we're on the topic of short-term memory loss, I (Cass) wanted to take this opportunity to tell you about one of my absolute favorite movies of all time. It's titled *50 First Dates*, starring what might be the greatest couple to ever grace the rom-com genre: Drew Barrymore, as forgetful Lucy, and Adam Sandler, playing the role of the unlikely romantic Henry.

I return to this movie time and time again because it's hysterical, and I get totally engulfed in the quirky but sweet love story of Henry and Lucy. The plot of the movie is simple. Henry, a smooth-talking bachelor who's terrified of commitment, falls head over heels in love with a girl he's just met. Her name is Lucy, and she's a gorgeous artist who happens to have a brain injury caused by a bizarre accident involving a cow in the middle of the road. And no, I'm not making that part up.

The unlikely couple meet at a local diner owned by a family friend of Lucy's. The poetic justice of a man who fears commitment falling in love with a woman who is incapable of remembering him in the morning is both ironic and hilarious.

Now, I know this might be a bit of a stretch, but I tend to find God in the most unlikely places—including but not limited to this movie. The parallels of this romantic comedy to the unconditional love of God are truly beautiful to me.

Just like Lucy's memory is erased nightly when she lays down to sleep, God keeps no records of our wrongs (1 Corinthians 13:5), and his mercies are new every morning (Lamentations 3:23). Even when we forget who God is or we wander away (Matthew 18:12–14), his steadfast love continues to pursue us daily (Psalm 136).

After spending most of the movie failing miserably at trying to replicate the experience of getting Lucy to fall in love with him, Henry finally decides to try something new. He creates a tape for her to watch every morning when she wakes up. It starts with him saying good morning, and gradually her doctor informs her of her accident, her closest friends and family gently remind Lucy who she is, and it ends with her and Henry's wedding day. Clearly, Adam Sandler isn't God—but the plot of this movie is so precious and reminds me of God's relentless pursuit of our hearts.

We might not be able to play a video for you every morning like Henry did for Lucy, but we hope this chapter serves you in the same way. Day after day, you can return to this section to submerge yourself in truth and gently write the Word upon the tablet of your heart (Proverbs 7:1–3).

A Gentle Reminder

We've mentioned this already, but we want to give you this gentle reminder:

> You aren't always going to *feel* free.
> You aren't always going to *feel* worthy or valuable to God.
> You aren't always going to *feel* like your life matters or that what you do matters.

But that's where faith comes in. Faith is knowing without seeing or feeling. Faith is believing what God says even if everything in your life is trying to convince you otherwise.

Life will try to beat the truth out of you—or, rather, the Enemy will try to beat it out of you through your circumstances. And we're here to encourage you to throw some punches right back at the devil. You hold the authority in Jesus' name, friend! Take the devil out to the parking lot and kick the crap out of him. Pick up your sword (the Word of God) and dispel the lies once and for all. He can't win. He may be vicious in his attempts, but he will never hold the victory. Jesus does.

Though the battle rages on, we proclaim victory from the trenches in the mighty name of Jesus. *It is finished* (John 19:30).

If you need to stick Post-it Notes on your bathroom mirror
to remind yourself of your worth in Christ, *do it*.

If you need to listen to the audio Bible all day to fill your
mind with his truth so there's no room for the Enemy's
lies, *do it*.

If you need to pray Scripture out loud to drown out all the
other noise, *do it*.

If you need to go for a drive, blaring worship music and
having a come-to-Jesus moment in your car, *do it*.

If you need to go into a secluded room to be alone with
God and renew your mind, *do it*.

To submit, you have to resist something else. So in our submission to Christ and his authority:

Let's resist what's not meant for us to dwell in.

Let's resist the devil and his attempts to draw us back into
deception and counterfeit identities.

Let's lay down our idols and toss out any fake or rotten fruit
that might be lingering in our lives.

Let's spend intimate time with God, undistracted,
unfiltered, and unfettered before him.

Remind yourself every day of this simple yet powerful truth
that your true worth isn't based on you or your circumstances.
It's not something you can work for, achieve, or accomplish. It's
not found in your status, appearance, or relationships. It's found
in one thing and one thing only: *Jesus*.

Her True Worth

We pray that you put this book down and it leads you to pick up the Bible.

We pray that when you turn the last page you will live life fully convinced and secure in who you are in Christ.

We pray that this liberating knowledge will be contagious, and you won't be able to keep it to yourself.

When you're finished reading this book, remember: *he isn't finished with you.*

The Worthy Woman Manifesto

This is who God says I am not:

    my past mistakes
    my failures
    my Pinterest-perfect home
    my greatest wins
    my success
    my appearance
    my social media likes
    my relationship status
    my flaws
    my roles
    my responsibilities
    my job
    my social media following
    my trauma

    my qualifications
    my income
    my status in society
    my rejection
    my abandonment

This is who God says I am (declare it out loud and live securely in it):

I am fearfully and wonderfully made.
    (Psalm 139:14)
I am God's masterpiece. (Ephesians 2:10)
I am made in his image. (Genesis 1:27)
I am forgiven. (1 John 1:9)
I am redeemed by God. (Ephesians 1:7–8)
I am called by my name, not by my sin. (Isaiah 43:1)
I am a new creation—the old life is gone.
    (2 Corinthians 5:17)
I am greatly loved by God. (Romans 8:31–39)
I am his child. (1 John 3:1)
I am an heir of God and co-heir with Christ.
    (Romans 8:17)
I am a member of God's family. (Ephesians 2:19)
I am blessed. (Ephesians 1:3)
I am chosen to be part of a royal priesthood, a holy
    nation set apart for God. (1 Peter 2:9)
I am his treasured possession. (Deuteronomy 14:2)
I am precious to God. (Isaiah 43:4)

Reflect and Respond

1. Do you struggle to remember your worth? How so?
2. If applying the Word of God daily is the key to remembering your worth, are you in?
3. What, if anything, stood out to you in the Worthy Woman Manifesto? Why?
4. Are you ready to live life free and fully convinced of your true worth in Christ?

Acknowledgments

Britt

Ryan, my wonderful husband. Your constant love, encouragement, and selflessness have been not only what made this book possible but what gave me the strength to push through and bring this book to completion. You're my person at the finish line, jumping up and down, shouting for me to keep going. You have gone to battle for me in prayer and have uplifted my heart when I've needed peace. You and I have shed so many tears of joy and excitement over how God is going to use this book. I will always admire how your heart burns for people to know Jesus and how you fight for the goodness of God. Thank you for always being obedient to where God is leading us and for shouldering at times what I cannot. You display the gospel in your actions and how you love without restraint. I am privileged and truly honored to be your wife and to serve the Lord hand in hand with you.

Ariana, my darling daughter. You have been my greatest blessing and reason for writing this book. Knowing that someday you will pick up these pages and gain a deeper understanding of your true worth and value in Jesus is the drive that kept me going through this entire process. I love you, sweetie girl.

Cass, where do I even start? Thank you for saying yes to writing this book with me. Thank you for partnering in ministry with me. Thank you for caring so deeply about this message and for fearlessly sharing the most vulnerable parts of your story in hopes that it sets someone else free. God is mighty within you, Cass, and I cannot wait to read more of your words to come. You are truly gifted with communication beyond belief. This ministry wouldn't be what it is without you, this book wouldn't be what it is without you, and I wouldn't be who I am in this very moment without you. I'm thankful for our friendship and sisterhood more than words can convey. (Hey. Look at us.)

Mom—my earthly mom and my spiritual mom. Thank you for believing in me. Thank you for being the God-fearing, Jesus-loving woman I've been blessed to be able to look up to all my life. Thank you for letting me hold your finger at Disney World so I could be fearless and explore but still know that you were right there beside me. You have always supported me, protected me, prayed with me, fought for my worth and value even when I didn't see it, and loved me with a Christlike love that I will forever be grateful for.

Dad, your incredible wisdom and understanding heart have led me through so many difficult times and through this entire process. No matter what, I know I can always count on you. Whether a phone call, a lunch date, or simply an ongoing back-and-forth of quoting our favorite movies together, you are always there, constant and steady in my life. You have cheered me on and have inspired me to be fearless in the pursuit of conveying this important message. You consistently challenge me to fight for what I believe in and to never settle for less than what God has planned for me. Thank you for who you are.

Ben and Nick, where would I be without the incredible and constant love and support of my brothers? I'm so thankful for you both and that God has so graciously given me such amazing siblings to grow in this life with. I don't know what I'd do without you two, and I appreciate how much you have shared your excitement for this book with me.

Nanny and Papa, you have given me the most precious gift: sharing the gospel with me and encouraging me to pursue Jesus. Thank you both for always being in my corner, showing me endless support and prayer, and teaching me about Jesus at a young age.

Nicole, you have shown up without hesitation during the most pressing times and have always been consistent in checking in with me during this process and making sure I'm taking care of me. Thank you for loving Ariana the way you do and for helping me care for her during the writing process. I'm so thankful for your loving and caring heart.

Rachael, I couldn't have done this without your constant loyalty to our friendship and keeping me laughing even through the harder times. And also sending me the best memes to keep my heart light.

Mallary, thank you for all our phone conversations when I've needed a break from writing. You've known me since I was thirteen years old and have seen just about every season of my life and stood by my side regardless. Your selfless, kind heart and your fierce mama love for your babies inspire me.

Angie, thank you for always celebrating with me and for offering such amazing wisdom and insight for this book. I love your heart for God.

Savannah, I'm so thankful that God brought you into my life. You have an amazing work ethic that encourages me to stop at nothing to get the job done for the Lord. Thank you for being such a wonderful friend.

Mariela, years ago we met on Instagram, and we were both in awe of what God was doing through us in ministry. And here we are now, writing books to set women free and spark a fire of passion in their hearts for the Lord. It's been a privilege to walk alongside you and to be able to share the excitement of this book with you.

Bethny, time and time again, God has used you to sow into me in my greatest time of needing His peace throughout this process. I'm truly grateful for our friendship.

Amy, you are not only a woman I look up to but a friend who has walked with me through one of the hardest pruning seasons of my life. Every single time I come to you for prayer, I know you got me covered. Thank you for being a warrior woman of God who inspires not only me but so many.

Pat Fig, you have a golden heart that I'm truly thankful for.

To the rest of my amazing family and friends, thank you all for believing in me and celebrating the importance and power of this message with me. I love all of you.

A special shout-out to the Waterford Starbucks for not kicking me out after writing in their café eight-plus hours a day.

Cass

I knew writing a book would be challenging, but writing a book during a global pandemic while raising three tiny humans, homeschooling, potty training, and with no family nearby was a legit miracle. God was able to use what little resources I had, where I was at, and produce this book. This book is proof that God truly does work in all things according to the good of those who love him and are called according to his purpose (Romans 8:28). The mercy of God alone sustained me through this process, and I'm forever in awe of how he carried me through.

To Dan Speer, thank you for loving me well. Thank you for daring to believe the dreams God planted deep within my heart and lending me your strength and belief when I felt like giving up. I'm grateful for your wisdom, tenderness, and leadership. Thank you for getting on the ground without hesitation to pray for me and with me for the hearts of the women who read these words. You're the king of the laundry mountain, the fun parent, and my favorite person on the planet. There's no one else I'd rather do life with.

To Britt, the visionary founder of Her True Worth, my ministry partner, coauthor, and dear friend. I'm grateful for the way you see the goodness of God within others, call out their gifts, and amplify their voices. The way you lead with humility and honesty inspires me. Thank you for partnering with me in

Acknowledgments

writing this book and pointing women to their true worth and identity in Christ. Your friendship is a gift I treasure. You're an anointed teacher and a brilliant artist, and I've had the privilege of watching you blossom into a courageous storyteller. I look forward to watching God continue to work within you and through you. (Who would've thought? Not me. But God.)

Mom and Dad, I'm truly grateful for your unwavering love and support. Thank you for being willing to enter into the conversations that led to the redemptive words written in this book. I will cherish those moments for the rest of my life. Thank you for helping me learn to embrace every part of my story. I'm proud to be your daughter, and I love you with all my heart. Moon and stars.

Keke, Poppy, and Steph, thank you for choosing to invest in my life and inviting me into your family when I was sixteen years old. I like to joke that I showed up and y'all couldn't get rid of me, but the truth is this: I know you wouldn't want to. Thank you for teaching me how to "adult" and always showing up. I'm grateful God brought you into my life. Love you.

Peggy and Papa Man, thank you for raising the man I adore. I'm grateful for all our soul-searching late-night chats on the couch, and I deeply value your wisdom in our lives. Thank you for pouring into us and always pointing us to the truth in all circumstances. We love you so much.

To my village of friends, both local and long distance, whose texts, voice messages, FaceTime calls, direct messages, group chats, Marco Polos, goofy GIFs, and prayers carried me through: Kaylee Shaw, Heather Yeldell, Whitney Ferringer, Bethny Ricks, Alexandra Hoover, Kayla Brint, Kelly Grantham, Toni Collier,

214

Ashley Abercrombie, Samantha Royer, Jess Connolly, Kennesha Buycks, Ariana Rivera, Mariela Rosario, Tabitha Panariso, Jennifer Lucy Tyler, Morgan Strehlow, Jackie Avales, Sharon Miller, Anna Mae Groves, Lisa Whittle, Baileigh Medlin, Hannah Schmitt, Emily Anne Gammon, MyLisa Thiels, Gretchen Saffles, Tara Sun Snyder, Grace Vernon, Sarah Hutcheson, Yuki Johnson, and Bailey Vinson. I'm so grateful to be surrounded by your love and support.

Last but certainly not least, Melody Janelle, Charlotte Grace, and Everett Daniel. Thank you for cheering me on as I serve God in ministry and in my motherhood. Girls, my sincere prayer is that you will always live confident and secure, knowing your true worth in Christ. May you never settle for less than God's best in all areas in your life. Your daddy and I treasure you. Everett, I pray daily for the woman you will one day decide is worthy of your heart. Until that day, Daddy and I will raise you to know your true identity in Christ and teach you to never lose sight of the inherent worth of others. I'm so glad I get to be your mom, and I love you dearly.

Special shout-out to OKC local coffee shops the Open Flame and the Underground. Thank you for keeping me caffeinated and motivated.

Together

We want to thank our dear friend Toni Collier. Your belief in the mission and message of this book helped bring it to fruition.

The way you lead and love inspires us. We're forever grateful for your friendship and support.

Our agent, Alexander Field, and our team at The Bindery Agency. From the moment we first met, we were confident that we wanted you to be the one to champion our words and help us point women to the hope we have in Jesus. Thank you for advocating for us and believing in us.

Our editor, Jenny Baumgartner, thank you for shepherding our hearts and this book with tender care. We're forever grateful for the way you've held our hands through this process and co-labored with us. Thank you for fortifying our words and fighting for our readers.

Our team at Nelson Books, thank you for investing in this book, catching the vision, bringing the message of Her True Worth to bookshelves and into the hands of countless women all over the world. We appreciate all your hard work and dedication.

Our Her True Worth community, thank you for allowing us to speak into your lives and point you to your true worth in Christ daily. It's a privilege we don't take lightly. We long for the day when we can meet you face-to-face, but for now we're grateful to be with you as you read the words on these pages. You inspired this book.

Our Her True Worth writing team: Aisha Diaz, Alexandra Hoover, Alexa Rodriguez, Amy Klutinoty, Amanda Sims, Annie Grossman, Kara Stout, Mariela Rosario, and Tara Sun Snyder. We couldn't do what we do without you. Thank you for being on our team and sowing generously into this ministry. Your words are laced with hope and speak truth into the hearts and lives of millions of women. We're honored to learn from you and to serve alongside you. You're the dream team!

Our Her True Worth community engagement specialist, Tara Sun Snyder. We're truly in awe of the way God continues to use your gift of communication and your love of community to bring him glory. We're grateful for your intentionality and creativity in cultivating the Her True Worth community.

Our Her True Worth devotional editor, Alyssa Chandler. Thank you for refining our words. Your contribution to the kingdom and the Her True Worth ministry is invaluable.

Our Her True Worth creative team: Bee and Diane and Isabela Schielke. Thank you for using your God-given creativity to share the gospel.

Our Her True Worth's marketing, branding, and website design extraordinaire, Samantha Royer. Thank you for capturing our vision and always being "here for it." We're so grateful for all the ways you've come alongside us every step of the way.

Ryan Maher, we're grateful for all of your techy expertise and hard work behind the scenes. You're the real MVP.

Notes

1. Angus Stevenson and Christine A. Lindberg, eds., *New Oxford American Dictionary*, 3rd ed. (New York: Oxford University Press, 2010), s.v. "affirm."
2. *Strong's Concordance*, s.v. H1966 ("Lucifer"), Blue Letter Bible (website), https://www.blueletterbible.org/lexicon/h1966/kjv /wlc/0-1/. See also Ron Rhodes, "How Did Lucifer Fall and Become Satan?" Christianity.com, February 7, 2022, https:// www.christianity.com/theology/theological-faq/how-did-lucifer -fall-and-become-satan-11557519.html.
3. *Strong's Concordance*, s.v. H7854 ("Satan"), Blue Letter Bible (website), https://www.blueletterbible.org/lexicon/h7854/kjv /wlc/0-1/; s.v. G1228 ("devil"), https://www.blueletterbible.org /lexicon/g1228/kjv/tr/0-1/.
4. Lexico, s.v. "praise," accessed March 1, 2022, https://www.lexico .com/definition/praise; s.v. "worship," accessed March 1, 2022, https://www.lexico.com/definition/worship.
5. Lexico, s.v. "approval," "admiration," "reverence," "adoration," accessed March 1, 2022, https://www.lexico.com/definition; emphasis added.

6. Trevor Haynes, "Dopamine, Smartphones & You: A Battle for Your Time," *Science in the News* (blog), Harvard University, May 1, 2018, https://sitn.hms.harvard.edu/flash/2018/dopamine-smartphones-battle-time/.

7. *VeggieTales: Madame Blueberry*, directed by Mike Nawrocki (Franklin, TN: Big Idea Entertainment, 1998).

8. Erin Heger, "Why Social Media Can Make You Feel Bad About Your Body—and 3 Easy Tips to Use Social Media to Boost Self-Esteem," *Insider*, November 5, 2020, https://www.insider.com/how-social-media-affects-body-image.

9. Holly Shakya and Nicholas Christakis, "Association of Facebook Use with Compromised Well-Being: A Longitudinal Study," *American Journal of Epidemiology* 185, no. 3 (February 1, 2017): https://doi.org/10.1093/aje/kww189.

10. Shakya and Christakis, "Association of Facebook Use with Compromised Well-Being."

11. Jonathan Haidt and Tobias Rose-Stockwell, "The Dark Psychology of Social Networks: Why It Feels Like Everything Is Going Haywire," *Atlantic*, December 2019, https://www.theatlantic.com/magazine/archive/2019/12/social-media-democracy/600763/.

12. Urban Dictionary, s.v. "cheugy," accessed February 27, 2022, https://www.urbandictionary.com/define.php?term=Cheugy.

13. Lexico, s.v. "self-care," accessed February 11, 2022, https://www.lexico.com/definition/self-care.

14. Lexico, s.v. "self-love," accessed February 11, 2022, https://www.lexico.com/en/definition/self-love.

15. Jess Connolly, "Shame Off You," Breaking Free from Body Shame Bible Study, accessed February 11, 2022, https://www.jessconnolly.com/biblestudy.

16. Elizabeth Dixon, "Breaking the Chains of Generational Trauma: We Don't Have to Pass Down Everything We Inherit," *Psychology Today*, July 3, 2021, https://www.psychologytoday.com/us/blog/the-flourishing-family/202107/breaking-the-chains-generational-trauma.

17. *Merriam-Webster*, s.v. "backsliding," accessed February 13, 2022, https://www.merriam-webster.com/dictionary/backsliding.
18. Bill Fay, "Key Figures Behind America's Consumer Debt," Debt.org, May 13, 2021, https://www.debt.org/faqs/americans-in-debt/.
19. "What Is Sanctification?" Got Questions Ministries, accessed January 31, 2022, https://www.gotquestions.org/sanctification.html.
20. Max Lucado, *He Chose the Nails: What God Did to Win Your Heart* (Nashville: Nelson Books, 2000), 103.

About the Authors

BRITTANY MAHER is compelled by love to empower women to simplify their identity based on one thing alone: Jesus. She is the founder of Her True Worth, a large and growing online community designed to liberate an entire generation of faith-filled women with the freedom found in discovering their true worth in Christ. She is also an evangelist with a burning heart for the broken and the lost. She and her husband, Ryan, invest most of their time in equipping and empowering God's people for digital evangelism across the globe. They believe in the importance of using every tool they can to help bring people to a saving knowledge of Jesus. Brittany is planted in Michigan with Ryan and their daughter, Ariana.

CASSANDRA SPEER is a popular Christian blogger whose heart is driven by the desire to see women discover the depth of God's love in a superficial world through the power of his Word. She is vice president of Her True Worth, a ministry created to encourage wounded and wandering women to find their identity and validation in Christ alone. Cassandra is passionate about sharing her faith and tackling the raw and messy moments of life with a little bit of humor—and a whole lot of Jesus! She is also the proud wife of an air force veteran. Cassandra and her husband are planted in Oklahoma City, where they live with their three children.

About Her True Worth

Brittany Maher and Cassandra Speer are the leaders of Her True Worth, a ministry that encourages women to find their identity in Christ alone.

If you're looking to explore the depth of God's love through his Word and discover your true worth with sisters by your side, then you've found the right place! We have the privilege of serving an online community of 1.6 million women worldwide and growing.

Follow us:

Instagram: @HerTrueWorth
Facebook: Facebook.com/HerTrueWorth

Looking to connect? Follow us on Facebook and join the Her True Worth Fellowship Facebook group. Search "Her True Worth Fellowship" on the Facebook app to join the group.

Her True Worth is a safe space for your heart to land, receive prayer, experience fellowship, and embrace sisterhood.

For more information about Her True Worth, visit our website at HerTrueWorth.com.